Hitched Horsehair

THE COMPLETE GUIDE FOR SELF LEARNING

Shoni Maulding

Hitched Horsehair: The Complete Guide for Self-Learning

by Shoni Maulding

Copyright © 1997 by Shoni Maulding

All rights reserved. No part of this book may be reproduced or transmitted in any form or by any means, electronic or mechanical, without written permission from the author.

Published by: River Publishing
                    P.O. Box 1123
                    Kettle Falls, WA 99141

ISBN: 0-9659624-6-6

Library of Congress Catalog Card Number 97-92318

Maulding, Shoni
    Hitched horsehair: the complete guide for self-learning
    p. cm.
    Includes appendix and index.
    1. Horsehair   I. Title
    2. Cowboys-Collectibles. 3. West (U.S.)-Collectibles. 4. Folk art. 5. Fiberwork.
    6. Arts. 7. Arts in Prisons. 8. Mexican-American folk art

10 9 8 7 6 5 4 3 2 1

Printed in the United States of America

Limit of Liability/Disclaimer of Warranty: The author and publisher have used their best efforts in preparing this book. The author and River Publishing make no representation or warranties with respect to the accuracy or completeness of the contents of this book, and shall have neither liability nor responsibility to any person or entity with respect to any loss or damage caused, or alleged to be caused, directly or indirectly by the information contained in this book.

Cover design by the Quinn Group, Spokane, Washington

Front cover photos: End of the Trail. Bolo and belt buckle are hitched inlays in sterling silver. Copyright © 1996, Shoni Maulding, Eagle and Double Eagle patterns.

Back cover photos: Baw's cane; End of the Trail. Belt buckle is a hitched inlay in sterling silver. Copyright © 1996, Shoni Maulding, Eagle pattern.

TABLE OF CONTENTS

What is Hitched Horsehair?	5

Chapter 1
    Overview of Learning to Hitch — 7

Chapter 2
    Buying Hair and Making Pulls — 9

Chapter 3
    How to Hitch — 13

Chapter 4
    How to Add, Drop and Stand Pulls — 21

Chapter 5
    How to Hitch a 6 Row Diamond — 27

Chapter 6
    Dyeing Horsehair — 35

Chapter 7
    How to Cross Hitch — 39

Chapter 8
    Number of Pulls Per Dowel Size — 47

Chapter 9
    Sizing of Hitched Horsehair Items – Belts & Hatbands — 51

Chapter 10
    Finishing Belts, Hatbands, & Key Fobs — 59

Chapter 11
    How to Use Graph Paper — 69

Chapter 12
    Leather Belt Ends — 83

Chapter 13
    Making Knots to Cover Joints — 93

Chapter 14
    Choosing Colors & Patterns — 99

Chapter 15
    The Horsehair Press — 103

Chapter 16
    Inlays — 107

Chapter 17
    Headstalls and Reins — 111

Chapter 18
    History — 117

Chapter 19
    Odds and Ends — 119

Chapter 20
    Complete Patterns and Directions — 121

Chapter 21
    In the Round Patterns — 169

Appendix
    Suppliers and Resources — 181
    Glossary
    Index

Dedicated to our Creator, Who makes all things possible,
and
To my husband, Ron, who has patiently supported me while this project was developed

Inspiration: Webster's Dictionary directly connects the Holy Spirit and human soul in its definition of inspiration.

I believe we are meant to glorify our Creator in every aspect of our lives. We can call on the Holy Spirit that is in us to guide us daily, to use our creativity, our minds, to teach us all truths. One of my ways is through hitched horsehair and writing this book. There are uncountable ways for each individual to express the workings of the Holy Spirit. Inspiration ➢ those flashes of thought, an insight into hitching, into life…..

ACKNOWLEDGEMENTS

To my husband, Ron, thanks for believing in me, knowing that I could learn to hitch and write this book. You have touched my life so much that there are no words to express it.

To my parents, Paul and Bette Peterson, who instilled in me a love of books and the written word. Thanks for letting us read at the dinner table.

To Ron's parents, Mel and Fran Maulding, thanks for helping build our house and proofread the rough draft.

To Sam and Ellie Henderson, thanks for learning hitching from the rough draft, the great meals, and good conversation and stories.

To Laura Golphenee, my friend and fellow student of life and our part on this earth, thanks for listening, helping with the photography, and your constructive comments.

To High Noon, Karen Kimball, Bev Klein, and Mark Margolis, thanks for letting us use photos of your hitched horsehair.

To Roberta Speer, Montana Territory, Whitefish, Montana, thanks for depending on Ron's judgment and ordering that first belt sight unseen.

Thank you to the companies and individuals who agreed to be in our appendix.

To Beth Shewchuk, thanks for proofing, grammar, and pushing an introduction chapter.

To Robin Stauts, thanks for computer help and proofing.

To Janis Kisman, thanks for your friendship, listening ear, and crucial paperwork help.

To our friends in the Kettle Falls area, thanks for listening as we went through the different phases of this book and house building.

To Mrs. Dodson, thanks for the good foundation of grammar and spelling.

To Helene Sage, thanks for letting me put your rein order on hold for a few weeks while we got this book to the printers.

To Alex Guier, thanks for computer help.

To Kim Ausland, thanks for over the backyard fence comments.

WHAT IS HITCHED HORSEHAIR??.....

Why buy something made from horse tail hair? Why is it a collectible art form? And considered high fashion? Add desirable to the list also. Not only that, it's functional.

Yes, hitched horsehair is all of these things and more. So really, what is it??

Horse tail hairs are twisted together into *pulls*. These pulls are knotted over string, and shaped to make belts, hatbands, headstalls, bridles, reins, bracelets, watch bands, key fobs, quirts, and earrings. Hitched horsehair inlays adorn belt buckles, bolos, barrettes, pins, spur straps, checkbook covers, wallets, vests, coats, boots, saddles, rifle slings, and guitar straps. Add canes and walking sticks to the list. Products created from this art form are limited only by your imagination.

Horse tail hair is a simple product, yet it produces beautiful and functional items. Descriptions of hitched items are inadequate. A person must see it to believe it. To see it, is to marvel. To produce it is mind boggling and incredible.

Hitched horsehair is a centuries-old art form, going back to the Moors who conquered Spain in the 8th century. The Spaniards brought it to the New World, where cowboys, Indians, Mexicans, sheepherders, and prison inmates have perfected this art.

This art form is time-intensive. These products cannot be mass produced as each one is individually hand crafted. There can be no short cuts in hitching a fine quality item.

Presently, few people have knowledge of hitched horsehair; even fewer know how to hitch. This book's purpose is to teach you to hitch and to increase your awareness.

Hitched horsehair is not just a craft, but a functional art form. It is different from other art because it is functional rather than just something to hang on the wall. It is eye-catching and a conversation piece. No matter what walk of life you are in, you can experience hitched horsehair in some way or another.

Our book takes you through the various stages of learning how to hitch – from the beginning to the finished product. The basics of hitching are simple. This book takes you step-by-step through hitching in order to arrive at competent ability in hitched horsehair. The refinement of this book and our experience goes beyond the scope of any current instruction available in today's marketplace. The secret to intricate designs is graph paper. Learn how to use graph paper and your designs will go from simple to complex very quickly.

Pictorials, such as eagles, End of the Trail, and buffalo, are advanced designs. These patterns are changing the scope of hitched horsehair. Today's hitchers are advancing techniques, products, and designs that go far beyond the traditional norm. We are *pushing the envelope* so to speak. Consider these advancements as historical, just as the old-timers developed this collectible art form.

So how valuable is hitched horsehair? Here's a story of one Montana family. The father owned a hitched horsehair belt and died. Did the siblings fight over who got the money, the land, or the other worldly possessions? No – just the hitched horsehair belt….

The knowledge and awareness of hitched horsehair as a desirable, collectible art form is increasing. This book's purpose is to enhance the Art of hitching. We hope you enjoy your travels through the pages as you create your own pieces.

We welcome your stories, photos, and informative comments. Let us know if we can use any of these in future publications.

And by the way, one of the sons acquired his father's belt, and promptly hung it on the wall as a piece of art.

Chapter 1

OVERVIEW OF LEARNING TO HITCH

This book takes you through the complete process of learning how to hitch. It goes step by step – from buying hair to the finished product. It is to your advantage to read through each chapter before attempting to do what is in that chapter. The chapters are in sequence with the basics of hitching first. A retired rancher learned to hitch from the rough draft of this book. He critiqued it page by page in 1996.

Suppliers of horsehair and other items are listed in the appendix.

Start with making a key fob. This is a small item, and gives you the feel of what hitching is about. It is the easiest project to complete. The technique of hitching can be done with something other than hair, such as string or yarn. However, if you're reading this book to hitch horsehair, then start with hair. Hair lays differently, and will be more pleasant to work with.

Patterns are based on a 6 row diamond. Learn the workings of the diamond, learn how to use graph paper, and the sky is the limit on what you can produce. We cannot encourage you enough on how much learning to use graph paper will enhance your patterns.

Hitching is a counting system, but you don't have to be a math expert to do it.

The cross hitch border is an edging that frames the hitching like a picture frame frames artwork. It looks like a barbershop pole.

While hitching, you'll be working with a tube shape. To flatten, see Chapter 15 on making a press. The chapter on leather ends covers both the leather work and sewing the hitching to the leather. Directions for traditional hand sewn knots are also in this book.

Whether or not you have ever created anything before makes no difference in learning to hitch. A desire to learn is the secret to successful hitching. Different steps in learning will be easy for you and harder for others, and vice versa. Anyone who hitches should be respected, no matter what skill level is achieved.

Skill is gained through repetition and time. Save all your hitched items and use them to see the progress you make.

Hitched horsehair is awe inspiring; it is humbling; it catches a person unawares. It is incredible that such beautiful things can be made from something so simple.

Learn by doing. Take each step knowing you can be successful at hitching. In life you learned to crawl, then walk, and then ride. Success in hitching follows this same concept.

There will be new terms to learn. These become familiar as you hitch your first key fob.

Your finished products are a source of pride – pride that you did it, that it looks good at whatever stage of hitching you are in. You will have a new respect of yourself, and your newly gained discipline.

Chapter 2

BUYING HAIR AND MAKING PULLS

This chapter focuses on buying horse tail hair, making pulls, preparing horsehair for hitching, and supplies.

Supplies

- Horse tail hair
- Non-inked, plain paper (for wrapping hair in)
- String or rubber bands

Buying Horse Tail Hair

Tail hair is better to use than mane hair due to its longer length. Hair is sold by the pound and tied together with string. These are called "bundles". Bundles may not be exactly a pound. When ordering, order in half pound to 1 pound increments. The supplier will try to match your request.

A good length is 25 to 28 inches. Longer lengths are more expensive. Shorter lengths require more adding when hitching.

White hair is more expensive than black or natural gray (also called mixed).

Suppliers of horsehair are listed in the Appendix.

Preparing Hair for Making Pulls

Hitching is done with hairs twisted together into a "pull". A pull is 10 or 11 horse tail hairs twisted together into a strand.

Look at the bundle of hair. Observe that the two ends are different colors and one end has thinner hair than the other. Hair at the bottom of the tail is thinner and a different color than hair nearest the animal's body. To have uniformity of diameter and color the entire length of each pull, hair must be taken from both ends of the bundle.

The bundle of hair will be divided in half and wrapped in non-inked, plain paper. (Do not use newspaper as ink can rub off on hair.) This prepares the hair for making pulls.

Take 2 sheets of paper about 4 inches shorter than hair length. Lay separately on a table. Cut the strings holding the bundle together. Take half the bundle in each hand, and slowly untangle the halves of the bundle from each other. Lay each half down on the separate sheets of paper. See Diagram #2-1.

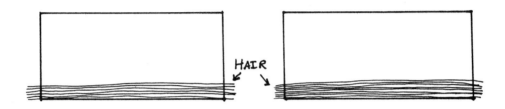

Diagram #2-1
Two Sheets of Paper with Half a Bundle of Hair on Each

Roll hair in paper, like a homemade cigarette. Use rubber bands or string in more than one place to loosely hold the paper around the hair. An inch or so of hair should be sticking out both ends. There are now 2 bundles of hair made from the original bundle.

Mark an "X" on the same end of the paper on both bundles to distinguish the difference between the hair colors and diameter.

Making Pulls

Pulls are individual hairs twisted together in a strand. Hair is pulled from opposite ends of the bundles to give uniformity in color and diameter.

Lay both bundles down, with the two marked ends opposite each other.

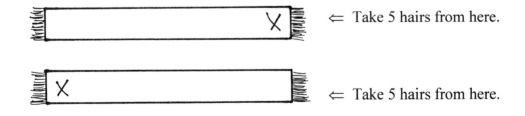

Diagram #2-2
Pulling Hair

Pull 5 black hairs from each of the bundles. ***PULLS CAN ONLY BE AS LONG AS THE SHORTEST HAIR, SO DISCARD ANY SHORT HAIRS.***

Knot the 10 hairs together as close to the end as you can. Hold the hair in two separate parts with the left hand. Using the right hand, twist the hair. Starting from the knot, roll the hair clockwise between thumb and forefinger. As the two bunches of hair twist together, move both hands down. Continue rolling the hair to the bottom end. See Photo #2-1

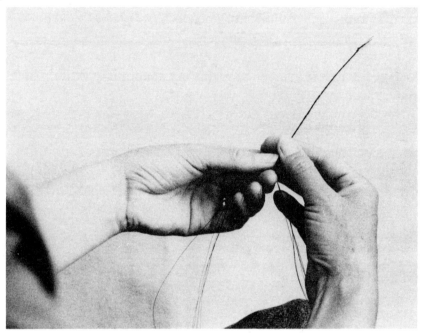

Knot the other end of the pull close to the end, making sure all hairs are caught in the knot.

White hair is thinner than black, gray, or mixed natural colors. Pull 11 white hairs, 5 from one bundle and 6 from the other, when making white hair pulls. This creates uniformity in diameter between different colored hair.

Natural gray (also called mixed color) and black hair will have 10 hairs per pull.

Tips

- Put white or black paper under the hair when pulling. Hair of the opposite color is easier to see.

- When twisting pulls, drape the hairs on opposite sides of your leg. This keeps the bottom end from twisting before the top end is twisted.

- If hands become too dry to twist hair easily, moisten hands with a wet cloth.

- **Pulls can only be as long as the shortest hair, so discard any short hairs.** Any short hairs will protrude from the finished product.

- Wash pulls with shampoo and water. The hair is usually dusty from sitting in warehouses and being transported. Hang to dry.

- Any combination of hair colors can be used in a pull. An attractive background is created by using 8 white and 2 black hairs, resulting in a beautiful gray. Remember, when mixing colors pull hair from opposite ends of the bundle. Also, adjust the amount of hairs for continuity in diameter.

- Discard any really coarse hairs or hairs that are abnormally white. These break easier and do not dye well.

- In our experiments with 27" gray hair, we made 1,586 pulls per pound of hair. This translates to enough pulls for 3 to 4 belts per pound of hair.

- Pulls made from 27" hair will hitch 4 to 5 inches when hitched over 2 strings.

Chapter 3

HOW TO HITCH

This chapter focuses on how to hitch, open hitch, closed hitch, and supplies and tools necessary for hitching.

Tools and Supplies

- Pulls of horsehair (see Chapter 2 on making pulls)
- Nylon string - #9 nylon twine, 2 spools
- Wooden dowels - $^3/_8$", $^1/_2$", $^3/_4$" in diameter
- Scissors or nail clippers
- Awl (optional)
- Ruler

Hitching

Hitching is a series of horsehair pulls knotted over string. The string is wound around a dowel for something sturdy to hitch over. The dowel also provides shape for the item to be hitched.

To get the "feel" of hitching, these first instructions will define how to start the first row, and open hitch and close hitch. Once this feels comfortable, go to the chapters on adding pulls, dropping pulls, and making a 6 row diamond.

Closed hitching is easier to do than open hitching. For your first key fob, consider doing only closed hitching to get the feel of hitching. This creates a spiral effect.

Alternating open hitch rows and closed hitch rows make straight rows instead of a spiral. Alternating open and closed hitch rows will be used with most hitched products.

Nylon string is better to use than cotton string because cotton string eventually rots over time.

Preparing the Dowel and String

Hitching will be done over 2 nylon strings laying side by side. Take 2 balls of nylon string, and knot together on the end.

Take a $^3/_8$" wood dowel at least 18 inches long. With a saw, cut a ½" long slit in one end of the dowel for the knotted string to hook in. Slip the string through the slit in the dowel, and pull until the knot catches and will not move. See Diagram #3-1.

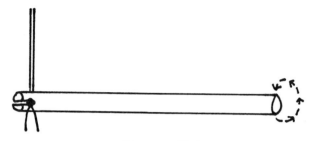

Diagram #3-1
Preparing the Dowel and String

If you do not have the equipment to make the dowel slit, then just tie the 2 strings on the dowel and secure with tape or a tack below the knot so the strings can lay next to each other. Keep constant tension on the string. To hold the string tight, put it around a table, chair, or bedpost. Then sit on the string. This provides tension.

Use your left hand to hold the dowel. The right hand will do the hitching. See Photo #3-1 (dowel is being held by the right hand for photo purposes only). Directions are for right-handed people.

When actually hitching, you will be looking lengthwise at the item to be hitched. However, the diagrams in this book are drawn as though you are looking at the item from edge to edge. The diagrams are drawn this way so you will be able to understand how to use graph paper.

Putting Pulls on String

One white pull and 18 black pulls will be needed for the first row.

Take a white pull to use as the *start point*. The start point is the first pull on the string. It is the starting count point of each row. This pull marks where the open or closed hitches start in each row. It is usually on the backside of the hitched object. Identify it in some way – either a different color as suggested above, or piece of tape or double knot on the end.

Pulls will be knotted on the string from one end. Fold over one inch of the white pull. This forms a loop.

Lay the loop under the string and pass the two ends through the loop. Pull on the 2 ends so the looped knot is against the string. See Diagram #3-2. (Diagram #3-2 shows the looped horsehair pull loosely knotted around the string so the knot can be easily seen.

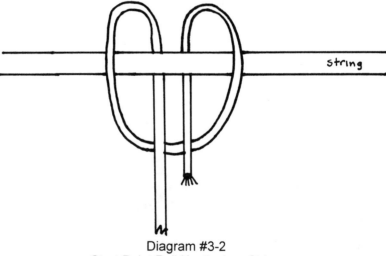

Diagram #3-2
Start Point Pull Knotted on String

The long end will be used for hitching. The short end will remain inside, against the dowel.

Holding closer to the middle, take a black pull, and loop and tie it on the string the same way the white one was put on. *HOWEVER, vary the lengths of the ends. One looped black pull now counts as 2 pulls on the string.* See Diagram #3-3. Ends of pulls must vary in length so new pulls will not have to be added all at the same time. Adding all at the same time creates bulges in the finished product.

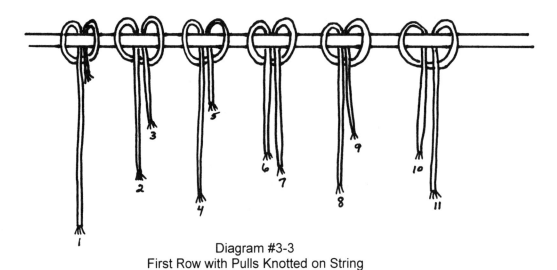

Diagram #3-3
First Row with Pulls Knotted on String

Loop and tie 17 black pulls on the string, making 34 pulls. Loop the last black pull with one end 1 inch long for #35 pull. (Do it like the white start point pull.) The white start point makes 36 pulls. Thirty-six pulls are the amount needed around a $^3/_8$" dowel.

Roll the dowel toward you, winding the string over the dowel until the pulls meet all the way around the dowel. Put the pulls to the extreme left (or top) of the string. See Photo #3-2.

You are now ready to start the actual hitching.

Chapter 3: How to Hitch 17

Open Hitch

Open hitch the white pull, which is the *start point.* Take the pull over the string, under the string, and up into the air. See Diagram #3-4.

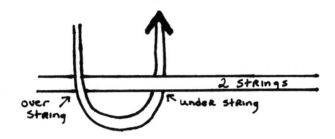

Diagram #3-4
Open Hitch

Pull the hitch up snug, but not tight enough to break the hairs. Open hitch the 35 black pulls, for a total of 36 pulls open hitched in the first row. ***HITCH THE PULLS IN SEQUENCE (that is #1, followed by #2, followed by #3, etc.).***

Closed Hitch

Close hitch the white pull, which is the *start point.* Take the pull over the string, back towards you, and under the string. See Diagram #3-5.

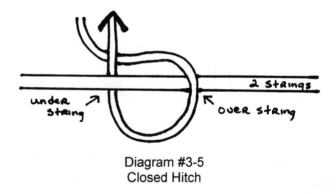

Diagram #3-5
Closed Hitch

Pull the hitch up snug, but not tight enough to break the hair. Close hitch the 35 black pulls for a total of 36 pulls closed hitched in the second row. ***HITCH THE PULLS IN SEQUENCE (that is #1, followed by #2, followed by #3, etc.).***

Continue open hitching one row, and close hitching the next row until you feel comfortable with open and closed hitching. OR, do only closed hitching for your first key fob. Closed hitching is easier and snugs the pulls down better.

Doing only closed hitching or only open hitching creates a spiral effect.

More Hitching Information

- Snug each hitched row down by pulling on each individual pull before hitching it. This lays the pull flatter in the previous row. It takes extra time, but there will be fewer pulls sticking up in the finished hitched blank.

- Do **NOT** hitch over knots on the pulls laying next to the dowel. Clip these knots when hitched rows are ½" away from the knots. Be careful that string, hitched work, and other pulls are not cut. Snug the dropped pull by pulling on the pull before clipping the knot off. This lays the hitched pull down flatter in the finished hitched blank.

- Pulls need to be dropped when there is about 2 ½" left on the pull. A new pull will be added in place of the old pull. See directions for this in Chapter 4 on adding and dropping pulls.

- Three inches of hitching makes a nice key fob. Finish the last row using directions in the next section. Set aside that hitching and start another item, or complete the key fob using directions in Chapter 10, *Finishing Belts, Hatbands, and Key Fobs* and Chapter 13, *Making Knots*.

Finishing the Last Row of a Hitched Item

The last row of the hitched item will be a closed hitch row because closed hitches are tighter and snug down better.

Begin with the white start point pull. Close hitch the pull. Then drop the pull by bringing it down under the string – the same way pulls have been dropped throughout your hitching (see Chapter 4 on dropping pulls). Close hitch the next pull, drop it; and continue this way with all the pulls until every pull has been closed hitched and dropped.

Cut the nylon strings coming from the 2 spools, leaving about 3 inches of string. Tie the 2 nylon strings together in a knot so the last row will not come off the string.

Leave the dropped pulls sticking out of the inside of the hitched tube. If this is a key fob, these dropped pulls will be a decorative tassel when trimmed and combed out.

When Mistakes Happen

It is inevitable that mistakes will happen, so learn from them, correct them, and go on with your project.

Use an awl to help unravel the pulls. Be careful that no individual hairs are broken by the awl.

Wetting the pulls helps unkink the hair if there are many rows that need to be taken out. Dip your fingers in water, put the water on the pulls, and smooth the hair out as you undo the pulls.

Tips

- Hitching is a counting system.

- Hitching over 1 string instead of 2 makes the pattern shorter, with more rows per inch. This takes longer to hitch. A good hitcher can do an inch per hour. This varies depending on the item's width and complexity of design.

- Leave at least 1 ½" to 2" of the pull laying alongside the dowel, both when adding and dropping. Anything less can work itself out of the finished hitched item.

- If the dowel is rough, use sand paper to smooth it. A wood sealant may also be put on the dowel to keep it from swelling up if water gets on it. Ask at any paint or craft department for an appropriate wood sealant.

- Pulls will lay flatter if they are *snugged down.* Before hitching a pull, pull on the pull. This makes the previous hitched row tighter and lays the pull down flatter in the previous row. Then hitch the pull. Also snug down each dropped pull before the knot is clipped. This does take extra time, but there will be fewer pulls sticking up in the air in your finished hitched blank.

- Individual hairs should not be sticking out. Reasons why they stick out:
    1. Pulls break while hitching and hairs stick up.
    2. When pulls are being hitched, the cut off dropped hairs get "pulled" up into the hitched item. Use an awl to put these hairs in the proper place.
    3. Pulls are made with short hair in them.
  If any hairs stick out, cut as close to the hitching as possible.

- If you do only open hitching or closed hitching, the rows will spiral instead of being straight. Experiment with this, using different colors. Alternating open hitch rows and closed hitch rows will make straight rows instead of a spiral. Alternating open and closed hitch rows will be used with most hitched items. Both spiral and straight rows are attractive.

- If you become confused as to whether you are open or closed hitching, look at the last pull and see which side of the hitch the hair comes out on. If it is on the side toward you, you are close hitching; away from you, open hitching.

- Hitch the pulls in sequence.

- To have more dowel to hold on to when first starting a project, cut a ¼" long slit at a 45 degree angle on the side of one end of the dowel, about 2" from the end. This replaces the slit cut in the very end of the dowel.

Chapter 4

HOW TO ADD, DROP AND STAND PULLS

This chapter focuses on how to add, drop, and stand pulls.

Adding Pulls

There are 2 reasons to add a new pull:

    1. A hitched pull is getting short and only has about 2 ½" left.

    2. A new color needs to be added in the pattern.

To add, simply lay a new pull under the string where you want it added. Leave about 1 ½" to 2 inches of the pull laying next to the dowel. The long part will be hitched in the next row. See Diagram #4-1.

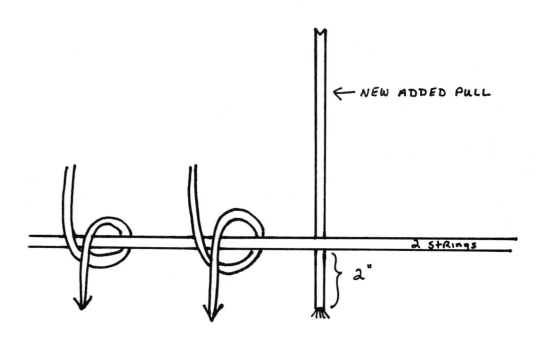

Diagram #4-1
Adding Pulls

Simple, right??? Well, there are a few other things that are necessary to know.

The following diagrams for adding pulls are based on a spiral design where all the rows are either open hitched or closed hitched. If you are hitching straight rows, the old pull will be dropped in Row 2. Then the appropriate open hitch or closed hitch knot will be done with the new pull in Row 2.

Adding Pulls in an Open Hitch Row

First, open hitch the old pull. Then add a new pull by just laying it in. Do *NOT* hitch the new pull in this row. In the next row, there will be 2 pulls coming out of the same hole – the short old pull, and the new long pull. Drop the old short pull first by bringing it under the string, pulling tightly, and laying it next to the dowel. Hitch the new long pull after dropping the short old pull. See Diagram #4-2.

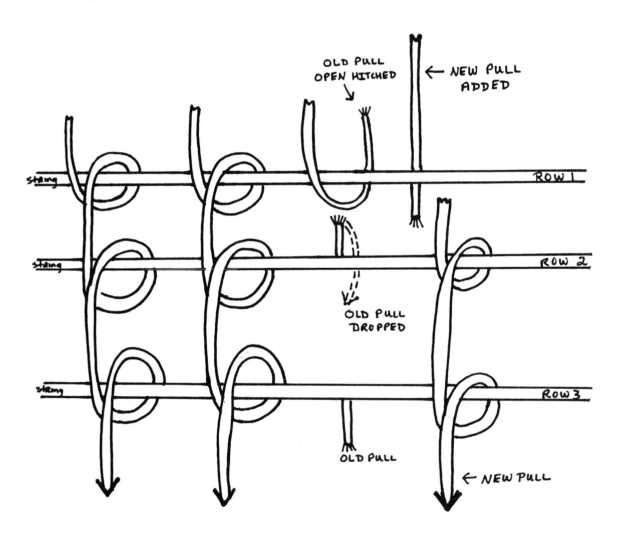

Diagram #4-2
Adding Pulls in Open Hitch Rows

Adding Pulls in Closed Hitch Rows

First, add a new pull by just laying it in. Then close hitch the old pull. Do *NOT* hitch the new pull in this row. In the next row there will be 2 pulls coming out of the same hole – the short old pull, and the new long pull. Drop the old short pull first by bringing it under the string, pulling tightly, and laying it next to the dowel. Hitch the new long pull after dropping the short old pull. See Diagram #4-3.

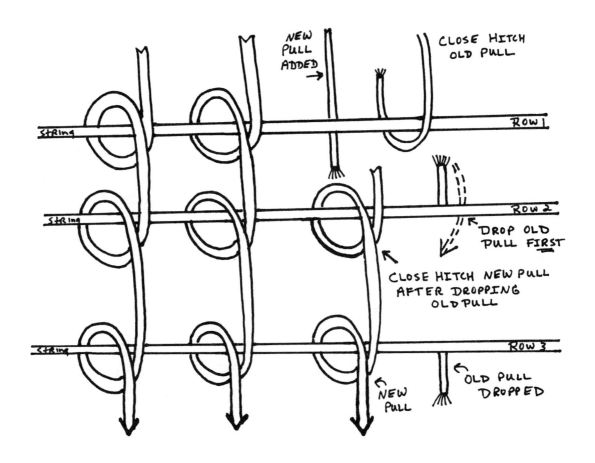

Diagram #4-3
Adding Pulls in Closed Hitch Rows

Adding Colored Pulls for a Pattern

The above directions for adding pulls work great for background colors. You want the longest possible pull to hitch with so the background seldom has to be added to.

However, the length of the colored pull added under the string can vary depending on the pattern to be hitched. For instance, one red pull can be laid about midpoint under the string. Half should be up and ready to hitch in the next row. The other half should be laying next to the dowel. This second half can be brought up and added when needed. This will make more sense when you start the 6 row diamond.

Adding Pulls Laying Alongside the Dowel

Pulls that have been previously dropped and are now laying down alongside the dowel can be brought up and added when they are the right color and length. Use only pulls close to where they need added. Pulls further from the add area don't work well.

Bring the pull up under the string. It is ready to hitch in the next row. Make sure that a dropped pull in a row is not used to add in that same row.

Tips for Adding Pulls

- Never hitch a pull in the row it has been added. Add the pull in one row and hitch it in the next row.

- When adding, always leave 1 ½" to 2" next to the dowel. These are your raw ends. If left too short these ends could work out and your hitching would come apart.

- Do *NOT* hitch over knots on the pulls laying next to the dowel. Clip these knots when hitched rows are ½" away from the knots. Snug dropped pulls before clipping knots.

- Avoid adding new pulls all at the same time, or bulges will be in the finished hitched item.

- Pulls of 6 inches or longer can be used. If there are just a few rows of hitching with one color, these shorter pulls can be used. When using shorter pulls, make sure they are long enough to do the pattern with that color. It is possible to add, but is easier to use the right length to start with.

Dropping Pulls

To drop a pull, put it under the string, pull tightly, and lay it along the dowel. It is not hitched. See Diagram #4-4.

Note: These are all Open Hitch Rows.

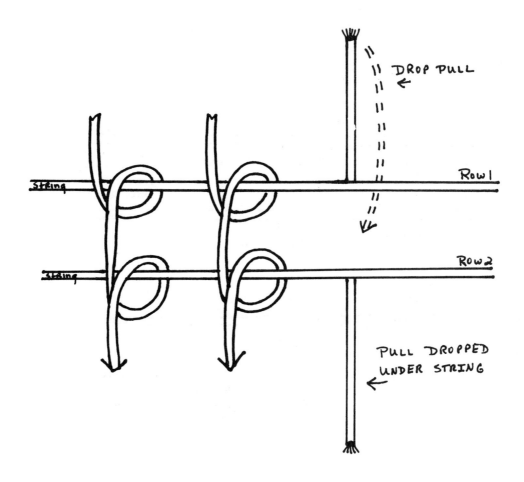

Diagram #4-4
Dropping a Pull

Standing a Pull

Nothing is done with the pull in that row. It is not hitched. It sticks up in the air, and is always dropped in the next row. It is the easiest part of hitching because nothing is done in that row with that pull.

Standing pulls are used extensively when hitching patterns. The 6 row diamond pattern will help make more sense of how standing is used. See Diagram #4-5.

Note: These are all Open Hitch Rows.

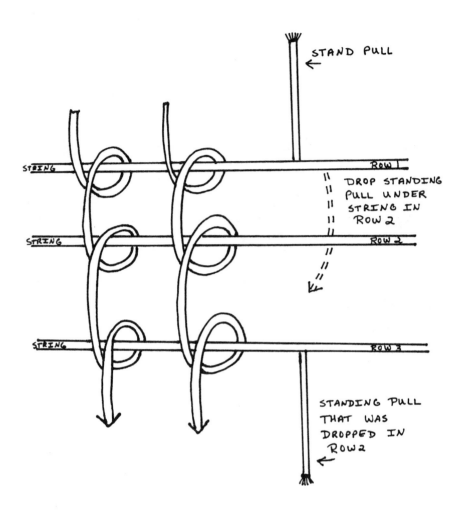

Diagram #4-5
Standing a Pull – Row 1
Dropping the Standing Pull – Row 2

Chapter 5

HOW TO HITCH A 6 ROW DIAMOND

This chapter gives directions on hitching a 6 row diamond. Most hitched patterns are based on a diamond shape. ***LEARNING THE 6 ROW DIAMOND IS THE BASIS OF HITCHING PATTERNS!!!!!***

The previous chapter on adding, dropping, and standing pulls is very important to know when learning a 6 row diamond. Refer to this if necessary.

When you start making your own patterns, refer back to these basic directions, especially when it comes to hitching the background.

There are modifications to these directions, but we think these directions are the best. These directions have stood the test in institutional use.

General Information

This hitching project will be on a $^3/_8$" dowel, with 36 pulls in each row. You will learn how to hitch a 6 row diamond with pattern colors of red, gold, and blue.

A white pull is used as the start point for easy identification. This white pull will be included in the background count. Therefore, when the directions say "X amount of black pulls to center", the white start point is included as a black pull. In actuality, there will be 1 white pull and 35 black pulls for the background. This is what you start with, and this is what you will end with when the diamond is completed.

ALWAYS START YOUR PATTERN ON AN OPEN HITCH ROW. This centers your pattern.

Basic 6 Row Diamond

Hitch ½" of background pulls, ending with a closed hitch row. The next row – an open hitch row – will be Row 1 of the diamond.

Row 1

    Open hitch 18 black pulls to center.
    Add 1 red pull.
    Open hitch 18 black pulls to start point.

Row 2

    Close hitch 17 black pulls to where 1 black pull and 1 red pull come out of same hole.
    Drop black pull that is in same hole as red pull.
    Close hitch red pull.
    Add 1 red pull.
    Stand next black pull.
    Close hitch 17 black pulls to start point.

Row 3

    Open hitch 17 black pulls to red pull.
    Close hitch 1 red pull.
    Add 1 gold pull.
    Open hitch 1 red pull.
    Drop standing black pull.
    Open hitch 17 black pulls to start point.

Row 4

    Close hitch 16 black pulls to where 1 black pull and 1 red pull come out of same hole.
    Drop black pull that is in same hole as red pull.
    Close hitch red pull.
    Close hitch gold pull that was added in Row 3.
    Add 1 gold pull.
    Open hitch red pull.
    Stand next black pull.
    Close hitch 16 black pulls to start point.

Row 5

    Open hitch 16 black pulls to red pull.
    Close hitch red pull.
    Close hitch first gold pull.
    Add 1 blue pull.
    Open hitch second gold pull (added in Row 4).
    Open hitch second red pull.

Drop standing black pull.
Open hitch 16 black pulls to start point.

Row 6

Close hitch 15 black pulls to where 1 black pull and 1 red pull come out of same hole.
Drop black pull that is in same hole as red pull.
Close hitch red pull.
Close hitch first gold pull.
Close hitch blue pull (added in Row 5).
Add 1 blue pull.
Open hitch second gold pull.
Open hitch second red pull.
Stand next black pull.
Close hitch 15 black pulls to start point.

You are now at the middle, or apex, of the diamond. Diamond colors will now be dropped, and background will be added.

Row 7

Open hitch 15 black pulls to red pull.
Add 1 black pull. (This goes in same hole with the last black pull that was open hitched.
Open hitch red pull.
Open hitch first gold pull.
Stand first blue pull.
Close hitch second blue pull (added in Row 6).
Close hitch second gold pull.
Close hitch second red pull.
Drop standing black pull.
Add 1 black pull.
Open hitch 15 black pulls to start point.

Row 8

Close hitch 14 black pulls to where 2 black pulls are in same hole.
Close hitch one of these 2 black pulls.
Open hitch the other black pull.
Open hitch red pull.
Open hitch first gold pull.
Drop standing blue pull.

Stand second blue pull.
Close hitch second gold pull.
Close hitch second red pull.
Close hitch 16 black pulls to start point.

Row 9

Open hitch 16 black pulls to red pull.
Add 1 black pull.
Open hitch red pull.
Open hitch first gold pull. (Both first gold and second gold will look like they are in same hole.)
Drop standing blue pull.
Stand second gold pull.
Close hitch second red pull.
Add 1 black pull.
Open hitch 16 black pulls to start point.

Row 10

Close hitch 15 black pulls to where 2 black pulls are in same hole.
Close hitch one of these 2 black pulls.
Open hitch the other black pull.
Open hitch red pull.
Stand first gold pull.
Drop standing gold pull. (Also called second gold pull.)
Close hitch second red pull.
Close hitch 17 black pulls to start point.

Row 11

Open hitch 17 black pulls to red pull.
Add 1 black pull.
Open hitch red pull.
Drop standing gold pull. (Also called first gold pull.)
Stand second red pull.
Add 1 black pull.
Open hitch 17 black pulls to start point.

Row 12

Close hitch 16 black pulls to where 2 black pulls are in same hole.
Close hitch one of these 2 black pulls.
Open hitch the other black pull.
Stand first red pull.

Drop standing red pull. (Also called second red pull.)
Close hitch 18 black pulls to start point.

Row 13

Open hitch 17 black pulls to where 2 black pulls are in same hole.
Open hitch the first of these 2 black pulls.
Drop standing red pull.
Open hitch 18 black pulls to start point.

In Row 13, the colored pattern has all been dropped and only background color is hitched. The standing red pull is dropped between the 2 black pulls that are in the same hole. There are 35 black pulls and 1 white pull which is what you started with in Row 1.

Continue with background color, or start another diamond. If continuing with background only, Row 14 will be closed hitch. Alternate closed and open hitch rows until the pattern is started again, or finish the item with ½" of background hitched pulls. See below for finishing the last row of a hitched item.

Remember to *always start your pattern on an open hitch row,* so the pattern will be centered.

To start another diamond right away and form a sequence of diamonds, follow these directions:

Row 13 – Alternative – Starting Another Diamond in Sequence

Open hitch 17 black pulls to where 2 black pulls are in same hole.
Open hitch the first of these 2 black pulls.
Drop standing red pull.
Add 1 red pull.
Open hitch 18 black pulls to start point.

Continue the diamond with Rows 2-13 of basic hitching directions for a 6 row diamond. When adding colors or background, use the pulls alongside the dowel if they are long enough.

Finishing the Last Row of a Hitched Item

The last row of the hitched item will be a closed hitch row because closed hitches are tighter.

Begin with the white start point pull. Close hitch the pull. Then drop the pull by bringing it down under the string – the same way pulls have been dropped throughout your hitching. Close hitch the next pull, drop it; and continue this way with all the pulls until every pull has been closed hitched and dropped.

Cut the nylon strings coming from the 2 spools, leaving about 3 inches of string. Tie the 2 nylon strings together in a knot so the last row won't come off the string.

Leave the dropped pulls sticking out the end of the hitched tube. If this is a key fob, these dropped pulls will be a decorative tassel on the end of the fob. For other projects, these dropped pulls will be cut off later.

See the next section on setting the horsehair with water. Let the hitched tube dry overnight. Slide the hitching all the way off the dowel.

Using Water to Set the Horsehair

When stopping for the day, dampen the hitching slightly with a spray bottle or whatever is handy. Then roll the hitching on the dowel back and forth on a flat surface (like a rolling pin). The water and rolling sets the horsehair hitches more firmly in place. Let the hitching dry on the dowel overnight.

The next day, slide finished hitching off the dowel until only about 1 inch is left on the dowel. A twisting motion back and forth works best in taking the hitched rows off the dowel. A vise is handy to hold the dowel while both hands slide the hitching off. *Be careful to not slide all the hitched rows off the dowel until the project has been completed.*

Continue hitching where you left off.

Tips

- Two pulls in the same hole are not necessarily a mistake. This can help identify what needs to be done with these pulls.

- As hitching is done, slide off the dowel. If more than 6" is on the dowel, it is hard to slide off. Do not slide all the hitching off the dowel until the project is finished.

- Putting the dowel in a vise aids in slipping hitching off the dowel. Both hands are free to slide the hitching off.

- Trim any loose hairs sticking out.

- If pulls cut into your fingers, put bandages or masking tape on those places.

- When adding colors or background, use pulls alongside the dowel if they are long enough.

- When mistakes are made and hitched rows are taken out, try the following to unkink the pulls: Wet fingers with water and rub on the pulls. Use just enough water to unkink the pulls.

- Terms and definitions that are used:

    "Going into a diamond" – Increasing the diamond pattern from the tip (or the start), to the apex of the diamond.

    "Going out of a diamond" – Decreasing the diamond pattern from the apex to the end (or bottom) of the diamond.

    "Building a diamond" -- Hitching the whole diamond pattern from start to finish.

- When you start creating patterns, think of the design in terms of diamonds, or partial diamonds. Instead of looking at the whole pattern, break it down into parts and find where the whole diamonds are. The pattern will start to look simpler in terms of hitching it.

Notes

Chapter 6

DYEING HORSEHAIR

This chapter focuses on dyeing horsehair, supplies needed, and mixing colors. It would be advantageous to read this entire chapter before dyeing any horsehair.

Supplies and Equipment

- Dye, RIT or Magma
- Hydrogen Peroxide
- White distilled vinegar
- Containers for mixed dye (plastic gallon milk jugs work well)
- Kettle to heat dye (hot pot works also)
- Measuring cups – 1 cup and ¼ cup
- Plastic silverware
- Plastic tub or a sink
- Shampoo
- Pot holders
- Cleanser, powdered
- Newspaper
- Funnel
- Plastic margarine containers
- Rubber gloves
- Plastic twist ties
- Dust mask or respirator
- Safety glasses or goggles

Hair Preparation

Pulls of hair will be dyed instead of individual strands. See Chapter 2 on making pulls. Usually only white hair is dyed, although natural gray can be dyed also. Fifty to 100 pulls can be dyed at a time. If a color is seldom used, dye fewer pulls. If you are experimenting with dye colors, dye just a few pulls.

For even coloring, peroxide the white pulls first. The solution to use is 1 part hydrogen peroxide to 1 part water. Mix this in a plastic milk jug and pour into a plastic tub. Put the white pulls in for 20 to 30 minutes, stirring occasionally to make sure all pulls are covered with the mixture.

Remove pulls from the peroxide/water mixture. Wash with warm water and shampoo to remove peroxide. Rinse till the shampoo is washed out.

Hang to dry, using plastic twist ties. Separate pulls for faster drying. Store and reuse the peroxide/water mixture.

Dye Mixtures

These directions use RIT dyes (easy to obtain) and gallon milk jugs, which is the easiest and most convenient way to measure and mix.

One cup white distilled vinegar will be used per 1 gallon of mixed dye. The vinegar helps to *set* the dye.

Cover work areas with newspaper to protect table tops. For health reasons, use a dust mask/respirator when working with dyes so the powder and steam will not be inhaled. Use safety glasses or goggles so the dye mixtures do not splash in your eyes.

Fill a gallon plastic milk jug up to the neck with water. Take out 2 cups of water. Throw 1 cup of water away. Heat the other cup of water to mix powdered dye in. Dissolve 1 package of RIT dye in the hot water. Add this mixture to the jug of water. Add one cup white distilled vinegar to the jug to set the dye. The vinegar replaces the water thrown away. Mix everything well.

Microwaves work great to heat the cup of water. Use plastic margarine containers to mix the hot water and dye in. Use plastic silverware to stir the water.

Put some of the mixed dye in a kettle, and bring almost to a boil. Watch carefully as it boils over easily. ***DO NOT LEAVE THE DYE MIXTURE UNATTENDED WHILE IT IS ON THE STOVE.***

Add horsehair pulls (50 to 100). Simmer (do not boil), stirring occasionally with a plastic utensil, and checking the color. Leave in dye bath until it is a shade darker than desired. Rinsing the pulls will remove some dye and lighten the color.

Remove pulls from dye and put in sink or plastic tub. Wash with hot water and shampoo to remove loose dye. Wash till water no longer discolors. Gradually rinse in cooler water. The final rinse should be in cold water. Shampoo should be rinsed completely out of hair.

Hang to dry.

RIT dyes can be stored and used again. If the dye has been stored, shake the mixture before using in the next dye batch.

Clean the kettle and any dye equipment with powdered cleanser after dyeing.

Pulls should be washed so well that colors will not bleed into each other in the final hitched product.

The amount of time in the dye bath depends on the color desired. Darker reds and yellows can take up to 15 minutes. Purples and blues can be as short as 2 minutes.

Dye batches will vary slightly in shades of color. Make sure you have enough pulls for an item before beginning to hitch. The next dye batch could be a different color.

Keep a record of the amount of minutes the horsehair pulls are in the dye bath. Use this record as a reference the next time hair is dyed. It is possible to dye the next batch close to the same shade of color; or lighten or darken the dye color with the next dye bath.

Some colors will not remain consistent with long periods of storage. We have found this with RIT yellows and neon pink. This may not matter if you do not want the same exact color.

Stronger mixes of dyes can be made, such as 1 package of RIT to 1 quart of water. This is your personal preference.

Common sense says to use pot holders when handling hot objects. Use rubber gloves to protect your hands from hot water and dyes.

Do **NOT** use any dyeing equipment for food preparation. This includes the kettle or hot pot, plastic utensils, measuring cups, and any other containers. Dye, both powdered and mixed, should be cleaned up immediately.

Mixing Colors

Experiment with mixing colors. This can be done with either the powder or mixing the liquids. When experimenting, dye just a few pulls. It's discouraging to take the time to pull 100 pulls and then dye in an ugly color.

Summary

Dyed horsehair adds much to the variety of patterns and the art form of hitched horsehair. This is where creativity and imagination can go wild. The hitched items can go from pastels to rich deep colors, from subtle to electric.

Experiment to your heart's delight. See Chapter 14 for ideas on colors.

Tips

- For consistency in color, always dye dry hair. Wet hair takes up the dye quicker. Results can be very different for the same time period if dyeing dry hair versus wet hair.

- Use a funnel to transfer liquids to milk jugs. To make a funnel, cut off the bottom half of an empty peroxide bottle. Use the top half for a funnel. Rinse well to remove peroxide.

- Explore other dye brands. Some have a short shelf life once mixed up of hours or days. Some do not dye hair well. Alternative dyes are worth checking into.

- To make gray, use equal proportions of colors across from each other in the color wheel; i.e. red and green, yellow and purple, blue and orange.

- To make brown, use colors across from each other in the color wheel, but do not use equal proportions. Use one color and add a bit of the other color until the appropriate brown is obtained.

Chapter 7

HOW TO CROSS HITCH

This chapter focuses on how to cross hitch, adding and dropping pulls with the cross hitch border, figuring out where the cross hitch border goes, and the basic 6 row diamond directions with cross hitch borders.

General Information

When cross hitching, pulls are crossed over each other. This creates a *barbershop pole* effect. This is the only time that pulls are not hitched in sequence. It is usually used on a belt or hatband edge. It finishes off the edges and gives the effect of bordering the pattern, just as a picture frame finishes off a picture.

Cross hitch pulls are added at the beginning of the hitching project.

Putting Cross Hitch Pulls on String

Select colors which are different from background colors when first learning. Loop cross hitch pulls on the string in the same way the start point pull is put on, with a long and short end. Four pulls on each border, for a total of 8 pulls, is attractive. But any amount of pulls can be used on cross hitching.

To distinguish which pulls are the cross hitch pulls, put 2 knots on the end (just as masking tape marks the start point pull).

How to Cross Hitch

Take the second pull and hitch it first. Then hitch the first pull over the top of the second pull.

Example: You have a white pull, red pull, white pull, red pull. Hitch the red pull first, then hitch the white pull. The white pull automatically crosses over the red pull. Hitch the red pull first, then hitch the white pull. The white pull automatically crosses over the red pull. All 4 pulls have been hitched.

Adding Cross Hitch Pulls

Add new pulls the same way that pulls have been added in previous chapters. Avoid adding new pulls all at the same time. Remember to add the new pull in one row, but do *not* hitch it till the next row.

Dropping Cross Hitch Pulls

DROP OLD PULLS FIRST BEFORE HITCHING ANY CROSS HITCH PULLS. This prevents slight lumps in the hitching.

How to Figure Where Cross Hitch Borders go on a Dowel

This example will use a $^3/_8$" dowel with 36 pulls on the dowel. There will be 4 cross hitch pulls on 2 borders for a total of 8 pulls used for cross hitch.

$$\begin{array}{rl} 36 & \text{total pulls} \\ \text{minus } \underline{8} & \text{cross hitch pulls} \\ \text{equals } 28 & \text{pulls for face and back} \end{array}$$

The face will have the colored pattern. The back will have the start point pull on it. Twenty-eight divided by 2 (for face and back) is 14. So there will be 14 pulls in the back, 14 pulls in the face, and 8 cross hitch pulls. This makes a total of 36 pulls.

Here is a chart to make the count easier:

Back

```
    7    6    5    4    3    2    1   36   35   34   33   32   31   30
8                                                                         29
9                                                                         28
10                                                                        27
11                                                                        26
    12   13   14   15   16   17   18   19   20   21   22   23   24   25
```

Face – Pattern is here

#1 is the start point. #1 through #7 are back pulls.
#8, 9, 10, 11 are the first cross hitch border pulls.
#12 through #25 are the face pulls where the pattern is.
#26, 27, 28, 29 are the second group of cross hitch border pulls.
#30 through #36, and #1 through #7 are the back pulls.

Tips

- Black and white makes an attractive cross hitch border, even when these colors are used for background. Marking the cross hitch pulls with 2 knots is especially important, so these do not get mixed up as background pulls.

- Cross hitch borders can only be used with straight rows of hitching where there are alternating rows of open hitch and closed hitch rows.

- The concept of cross hitch can be used as a decorative effect on spiral hitching or as part of a face pattern.

Basic Directions for a 6 Row Diamond with Cross Hitch Borders

Following are the basic directions for a 6 row diamond with 2 cross hitch borders. This will be done on a $3/8$" dowel with 36 pulls. These are the same directions you have been using to make a 6 row diamond, except these have the cross hitch border.

Pulls should be added in the following order, using a black background and red and white for the cross hitch border:

> 1 white pull as the start point. It is counted as a black background pull.
> 6 black pulls – background in back
> 1 white pull – cross hitch
> 1 red pull – cross hitch
> 1 white pull – cross hitch
> 1 red pull – cross hitch
> 14 black pulls – background of face where pattern is
> 1 white pull – cross hitch
> 1 red pull – cross hitch
> 1 white pull – cross hitch
> 1 red pull – cross hitch
> 7 black pulls – background in back

Before beginning the 6 row diamond, hitch ½" as follows, with alternating open and closed hitch rows:

Open Hitch Row:
> Open hitch 7 black pulls to cross hitch border. (White start point pull is counted as a black pull.)
> Open hitch 1 red cross hitch pull.
> Open hitch 1 white cross hitch pull.
> Open hitch 1 red cross hitch pull.
> Open hitch 1 white cross hitch pull.
> Open hitch 14 black pulls. (Face pulls where pattern will be.)

Open hitch 1 red cross hitch pull.
Open hitch 1 white cross hitch pull.
Open hitch 1 red cross hitch pull.
Open hitch 1 white cross hitch pull.
Open hitch 7 black pulls to start point.

Close Hitch Row

Close hitch 7 black pulls to cross hitch border.
Close hitch 1 white cross hitch pull.
Close hitch 1 red cross hitch pull.
Close hitch 1 white cross hitch pull.
Close hitch 1 red cross hitch pull.
Close hitch14 black pulls. (Face pulls.)
Close hitch 1 white cross hitch pull.
Close hitch 1 red cross hitch pull.
Close hitch 1 white cross hitch pull.
Close hitch 1 red cross hitch pull.
Close hitch 7 black pulls to start point.

Row 1 – Starting the 6 row diamond pattern

Open hitch 7 black pulls to cross hitch border. (White start point pull is counted as a black pull.)
Open hitch 4 cross hitch pulls.
Open hitch 7 black pulls to center.
Add 1 red pull.
Open hitch 7 black pulls to cross hitch border.
Open hitch 4 cross hitch pulls.
Open hitch 7 black pulls to start point.

Row 2

Close hitch 7 black pulls to cross hitch border.
Close hitch 4 cross hitch pulls.
Close hitch 6 black pulls to where 1 black pull and 1 red pull come out of same hole.
Drop black pull that is in same hole as red pull.
Close hitch red pull.
Add 1 red pull.
Stand next black pull.
Close hitch 6 black pulls to cross hitch border.
Close hitch 4 cross hitch pulls.
Close hitch 7 black pulls to start point.

Row 3

Open hitch 7 black pulls to cross hitch border.
Open hitch 4 cross hitch pulls.
Open hitch 6 black pulls to red pull.
Close hitch 1 red pull.
Add 1 gold pull.
Open hitch 1 red pull.
Drop standing black pull.
Open hitch 6 black pulls to cross hitch border.
Open hitch 4 cross hitch pulls.
Open hitch 7 black pulls to start point.

Row 4

Close hitch 7 black pulls to cross hitch border.
Close hitch 4 cross hitch pulls.
Close hitch 5 black pulls to where 1 black pull and 1 red pull come out of same hole.
Drop black pull that is in same hole as red pull.
Close hitch red pull.
Close hitch gold pull that was added in row 3.
Add 1 gold pull.
Open hitch red pull.
Stand next black pull.
Close hitch 5 black pulls to cross hitch border.
Close hitch 4 cross hitch pulls.
Close hitch 7 black pulls to start point.

Row 5

Open hitch 7 black pulls to cross hitch border.
Open hitch 4 cross hitch pulls.
Open hitch 5 black pulls to red pull.
Close hitch red pull.
Close hitch first gold pull.
Add 1 blue pull.
Open hitch second gold pull (added in row 4).
Open hitch second red pull.
Drop standing black pull.
Open hitch 5 black pulls to cross hitch border.
Open hitch 4 cross hitch pulls.
Open hitch 7 black pulls to start point.

Row 6

Close hitch 7 black pulls to cross hitch border.
Close hitch 4 cross hitch pulls.
Close hitch 4 black pulls to where 1 black pull and 1 red pull come out of same hole.
Drop black pull that is in same hole as red pull.
Close hitch red pull.
Close hitch first gold pull.
Close hitch blue pull (added in row 5).
Add 1 new blue pull.
Open hitch second gold pull.
Open hitch second red pull.
Stand next black pull.
Close hitch 4 black pulls to cross hitch border.
Close hitch 4 cross hitch pulls.
Close hitch 7 black pulls to start point.

Row 7

Open hitch 7 black pulls to cross hitch border.
Open hitch 4 cross hitch pulls.
Open hitch 4 black pulls to red pull.
Add 1 black pull.
Open hitch red pull.
Open hitch first gold pull.
Stand first blue pull.
Close hitch second blue pull. (added in row 6).
Close hitch second gold pull.
Close hitch second red pull.
Drop standing black pull.
Add 1 new black pull.
Open hitch 4 black pulls to cross hitch border.
Open hitch 4 cross hitch pulls.
Open hitch 7 black pulls to start point.

Row 8

Close hitch 7 black pulls to cross hitch border.
Close hitch 4 cross hitch pulls.
Close hitch 3 black pulls to where 2 black pulls are in same hole.
Close hitch one of these 2 black pulls.
Open hitch the other black pull.
Open hitch red pull.
Open hitch first gold pull.

Drop standing blue pull.
Stand second blue pull.
Close hitch second gold pull.
Close hitch second red pull.
Close hitch 5 black pulls to cross hitch border.
Close hitch 4 cross hitch pulls.
Close hitch 7 black pulls to start point.

Row 9

Open hitch 7 black pulls to cross hitch border.
Open hitch 4 cross hitch pulls.
Open hitch 5 black pulls to red pull.
Add 1 black pull.
Open hitch red pull.
Open hitch first gold pull.
Drop standing blue pull.
Stand second gold pull.
Close hitch second red pull.
Add 1 black pull.
Open hitch 5 black pulls to cross hitch border.
Open hitch 4 cross hitch pulls.
Open hitch 7 black pulls to start point.

Row 10

Close hitch 7 black pulls to cross hitch border.
Close hitch 4 cross hitch pulls.
Close hitch 4 black pulls to where 2 black pulls are in same hole.
Close hitch one of these 2 black pulls.
Open hitch the other black pull.
Open hitch red pull.
Stand first gold pull.
Drop standing gold pull.
Close hitch second red pull.
Close hitch 6 black pulls to cross hitch border.
Close hitch 4 cross hitch pulls.
Close hitch 7 black pulls to start point.

Row 11

Open hitch 7 black pulls to cross hitch border.
Open hitch 4 cross hitch pulls.
Open hitch 6 black pulls to red pull.
Add 1 black pull.

Open hitch red pull.
Drop standing gold pull.
Stand second red pull.
Add 1 black pull.
Open hitch 6 black pulls to cross hitch border.
Open hitch 4 cross hitch pulls.
Open hitch 7 black pulls to start point.

Row 12

Close hitch 7 black pulls to cross hitch border.
Close hitch 4 cross hitch pulls.
Close hitch 5 black pulls to where 2 black pulls are in same hole.
Close hitch one of these 2 black pulls.
Open hitch the other black pull.
Stand first red pull.
Drop standing red pull.
Close hitch 7 black pulls to cross hitch border.
Close hitch 4 cross hitch pulls.
Close hitch 7 black pulls to start point.

Row 13

Open hitch 7 black pulls to cross hitch border.
Open hitch 4 cross hitch pulls.
Open hitch 6 black pulls to where 2 black pulls are in same hole.
Open hitch the first of these 2 black pulls.
Drop standing red pull.
Open hitch other black pull in same hole.
Open hitch 6 black pulls to cross hitch border.
Open hitch 4 cross hitch pulls.
Open hitch 7 black pulls to start point.

Row 14

Close hitch 7 black pulls to cross hitch border.
Close hitch 4 cross hitch pulls.
Close hitch 14 black pulls to cross hitch border.
Close hitch 4 cross hitch pulls.
Close hitch 7 black pulls to start point.

Continue with background or start a new pattern.

Chapter 8

NUMBER OF PULLS PER DOWEL SIZE

This chapter has charts on how many pulls per dowel size, and suggestions on which dowel size is best for which projects.

Dowel Size and Number of Pulls

These charts are based on 10 hairs for each pull of black and natural gray hair; and 11 hairs for each white hair pull. If fewer or more hairs per pull are used, adjustments will have to be made.

The dowel size is determined by its diameter and sold that way.

Size of Dowel	Number of Total Pulls	Number of Face Pulls
1 inch	96	
$7/8$ inch	84	38
$3/4$ inch	72	32
$5/8$ inch	60	26
$1/2$ inch	52	22
$3/8$ inch	36	14
$1/4$ inch	24	8
$3/16$ inch	18	
$1/8$ inch	16	

Suggested Sizes of Dowels – Belts

Belts are best made with ¾", ⅝", and ½" size dowels.

Children's belts are best made with ⅜" size dowels. Most people will not buy a child's belt due to the price.

This chart gives the approximate finished (or pressed) width of the item. Remember these are approximate widths. The pressed width is approximately twice the size of the dowel.

Size of Dowel	Width of Finished (or Pressed) Item
$7/8$ inch	1 ¾ inches
¾ inch	1 $3/8$ inches
$5/8$ inch	1 ¼ inches
½ inch	1 inch
$3/8$ inch	¾ inch

Belts are usually referred to by their width in inches.

A 1 $3/8$ inch wide belt is sometimes called a 1 ½" belt. This is because ¾ multiplied by 2 is 1 ½ inches. It is also referred to as a *man's belt* because men are generally the ones who buy this width. This width usually does not go through belt loops of most men's dress pants and women's pants. Men's jeans have loops to accommodate this belt width.

The 1 ¼ inch wide belt is good for men who want a belt that will fit all their pants, and women who want something wider.

Most women order the 1 inch wide belt.

Belts wider than 1 $3/8$ inches look out of balance (author's personal opinion).

Suggested Sizes – Hatbands

Hatbands can be either pressed flat like belts, or left "in the round".

If pressed, hitch around the $3/8$" dowel, for a finished width of ¾ inches (sometimes closer to $7/8$ inches).

If left in the round, hitch around the $3/8$ dowel, or a $3/16$ or ¼ inch nylon rope. If hitching around rope, see Chapter 17 on making reins.

Suggested Sizes – Headstalls

If pressed, hitch around the $3/8$ inch dowel, for a finished width of ¾ inches (sometimes closer to $7/8$ inches).

If left in the round, hitch over $3/16$ inch nylon rope.

Suggested Sizes – Reins

Hitch over $3/16$ inch nylon rope. We have hitched over ¼ inch rope, but the reins were too bulky.

Suggested Sizes – Inlays

Inlays can be hitched over any size dowel, depending on what is required for the finished pressed width.

Remember that the hitched tube can be cut either before or after being pressed. See Chapter 16 on inlays.

Bracelets

Metal tubing (or rods) can be hitched over for bracelets. The tubing is left inside so the metal can be formed to the wrist. Choose metal and metal diameters that can be bent.

Tips

- Wood dowels smaller in diameter than ¼ inch are easily broken. If using smaller diameters, use metal tubing (or rods).

- Plastic PVC pipe can also be hitched over. Some prisons and correctional facilities will approve hitched horsehair in their Hobby Programs if PVC is used instead of wood dowels.

- If using small diameter dowels, there is the option of having less hair in each pull. The amount of pulls in each row would have to be adjusted.

- With smaller diameter dowels, smaller string may be used to hitch over.

- Earrings are not necessarily an easy item to make. They are usually hitched over small diameters, with smaller string and fewer hairs per pull.

Notes

Chapter 9

Sizing of Hitched Horsehair Items Belts & Hatbands

This chapter focuses on lengths and widths of the hitched blank, the finished lengths and widths of belts and hatbands, and how to measure for these.

It would be beneficial to read this entire chapter through before starting a belt. Information on belts will be covered first.

General Information

Ideally, the belt size measurement should go from the fold over where the buckle is attached, to the center hole of the five punched holes. See Diagram #9-1.

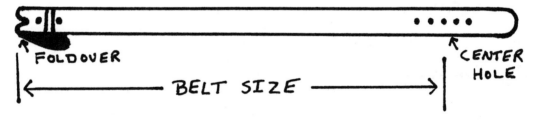

Diagram #9-1
Belt Size Measurement

Belts made following the directions in this book will follow this criteria. A standard buckle length of 1 ½" is used in these directions.

Buckle sizes, leather ends, and the finished hitched blank all play a part in the finished belt size.

The finished hitched blank is what was hitched and will be sewn to the leather ends. Both the leather ends and the hitched blank make the finished belt.

An accurate belt size centers the hitched blank in the person's back, so all these measurements are important.

Taking Measurements for a Belt Size

Belt sizes are *NOT* the waist size. It's easy to use these sizes interchangeably, but they are not the same thing.

Before measuring, understand that a cloth tape measure can stretch, so it is not always accurate. However, it follows the contour of what you're measuring; so it's the easiest to measure with. After measuring with a cloth tape, put the cloth tape against a metal or wood yardstick to get the accurate measurement.

Both the belt and buckle sizes need to be taken into consideration with a belt length.

There are 3 methods to take a belt size:

⇒ Take a belt the person is already wearing. Measure from the fold over where the buckle is attached, to the buckle hole used most often. Follow the contours of the old belt.

This is the easiest and most accurate way to get a belt measurement.

⇒ Take the pants waist size, and add 2 inches.

This works especially well for men because their pants waist size is how pants are bought. It's harder for women to use this method as most pants are not measured by waist size.

⇒ Measure around the waist (clothes on). Pull the tape snug, but not too tight.

Remember to convert the cloth tape measurement to a metal or wood yardstick.

Measuring the Buckle

Most buckles are a standard 1 ½" in length. These basic directions for figuring the hitched blank length and leather ends use the standard 1 ½" buckle length. However, some buckles are longer or shorter in length. This will affect the hitched blank length.

Diagram #9-2 shows how to measure the buckle length. These are the two most common types of buckles.

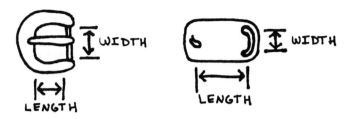

Diagram #9-2
Buckle Lengths and Widths

If the buckle length is 1 ½", take the belt size from one of the 3 methods described above.

If the buckle length is longer or shorter than 1 ½", adjustments will have to be made when figuring the hitched blank length. This is covered in the section on *Buckles Shorter or Longer than 1 ½" in Length* in this chapter. Beaded buckles or rodeo buckles tend to be different.

Tips on Measuring Belt Sizes

- Five holes will be punched in the leather end for the buckle to be hooked into. Ideally the buckle should hook into the center hole of these five holes. This will center the hitched blank in the middle of the person's back.

- When measuring the finished belt, the belt size measurement should go from the fold over where the buckle is attached, to the center hole of the five punched holes. This is using a standard buckle length of 1 ½". Other buckle lengths will make this longer or shorter.

- The holes on either side of the center hole are handy for a person losing or gaining weight. Different pants can also fit higher or lower on the body, and a hole other than the center hole will be used. The hitched blank would then be off center, but you have no control over that.

Figuring Lengths of Hitched Blanks

The finished hitched blank is what was hitched and will be sewn to the leather ends. It is usually different from what was actually hitched. See the next section to clarify this.

Determining a finished hitched blank: Take the belt size, and subtract 6 inches. Example: A 32" belt size minus 6" equals a 26" finished hitched blank.

This hitched blank uses a standard buckle length of 1 ½". See below for further instructions if the buckle length is shorter or longer.

Where does this 6" go?? The leather belt ends make up the other 6". There will be 3" of leather on either side of the hitched blank. Three inches will be from the fold over to the hitched blank. Three inches will be from the center hole to the hitched blank. See Diagram #9-3.

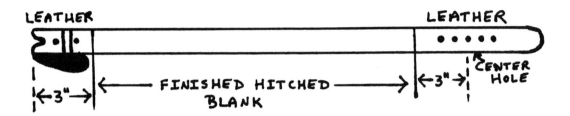

Diagram #9-3
Belt Measurements

Some of the leather and hitched blank on the front side will be under knots or leather covering the joint where these two are sewn together. Even though the joints are covered, this area is in the final belt sizing. Remember this, or your belt size will be wrong. If it's easier, just visualize the leather and hitched blank without the joints covered.

Finished Hitched Blank and Actual Hitched Blank

We keep referring to the finished hitched blank. The finished hitched blank is the hitched horsehair that is sewn to leather ends.

The actual hitched blank is the part that was really hitched, put in the press, with nothing cut off.

The actual hitching may be longer or shorter than what is needed.

If the blank is shorter, there are 3 ways to deal with this:

⇒ Hitch another blank. Do *NOT* try to stretch the short one to make it longer. It won't stretch enough to compensate for the needed extra length; and it can damage the hitched rows.

⇒ If the hitching is not completed, extra background or patterns may be added. See Chapter 11, *How to Use Graph Paper,* for more detail.

⇒ Put on longer leather belt ends.

Extremely long leather ends make the entire belt look unbalanced. The customer is paying for a hitched horsehair belt. To maintain high quality products, give the customer what he's paying for. Option #3, putting on longer belt ends, for dealing with a short blank is not the best option.

The **BEST WAY** is to hitch a longer blank to start with. Always plan to hitch one inch more than the required finished hitched blank.

Using the example above: 32" belt size minus 6" for the belt ends equals a finished hitched blank of 26". Therefore, actually hitch 27".

One inch is added due to
1) Shrinkage when the blank is pulled off the dowel.
2) Variations in pattern and background estimates.
3) Cutting off the first and last rows.

The chapter on graph paper covers the pattern variation estimates.

Hitched blanks and leather ends both need to be high quality for an overall good product. If one or the other look bad, the whole item will look bad.

If the customer wants more leather showing, adjust the hitched blank accordingly.

Buckles Shorter or Longer than 1 ½"

If a buckle length is shorter or longer than 1 ½", adjustments have to be made in the finished hitched blank. This keeps the correct belt size.

Using examples will best explain this.

A buckle length is 2". That is ½" more than the standard buckle size of 1 ½". Therefore, subtract 6 ½" from the belt size for the finished hitched blank.

When there is a longer buckle length, a shorter hitched blank is needed.

A buckle length is 1". That is ½" less than the standard buckle size of 1 ½". Therefore, subtract 5 ½" from the belt size for the finished hitched blank.

When there is a shorter buckle length, a longer hitched blank is needed.

Belt Loops or Keepers

Most keepers are ¼" or ³/₈" in length. See Diagram #9-4 for measuring keepers.

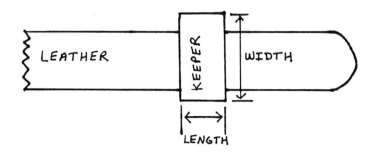

Diagram #9-4
Measuring Keepers

If keepers are abnormally long, or if there is more than one keeper, adjustments will have to be made with the leather and hitched blank. The hitched blank will be shorter, and leather ends longer to accommodate the keeper.

Belt Widths

The best widths for belts are 1", 1 ¼", and 1 ³/₈" (also called 1 ½").

Women usually order 1" wide as it goes through all their belt loops (jeans and dress pants).

The 1 ¼" width is good for women and men. It fits through men's dress pants better than 1 ³/₈".

The 1 ³/₈" width is usually what men will order, especially men who wear primarily jeans.

Belts can be made any width. The ¾" wide would be for petite people or children. Most people will not pay these prices for a child's belt.

A 2" belt can be made, but the author's personal opinion is that this width looks unbalanced.

More detailed information on dowel size and number of pulls for these widths is in Chapter 8, *Number of Pulls Per Dowel Size.*

Hatbands

A 21 inch finished hitched blank is a standard size. Some hitchers will look down on anything shorter. Remember to actually hitch 22 inches to allow for shrinkage, pattern estimates, and cutting off the first and last rows.

A hatband can be finished with leather ends, or horsehair ends with a slider knot. See Chapter 10, *Finishing Belts, Hatbands, and Key Fobs,* for this information.

A good width is ¾" wide if the hatband is pressed. Or hitch over $^3/_{16}$" or ¼" rope. See Chapter 8, *Number of Pulls Per Dowel Size*, for more information on hatbands.

If the hatband is hitched over rope, hitch only 21 inches. The rope remains inside. No hitching will be cut off.

Notes

Chapter 10

FINISHING BELTS, HATBANDS, AND KEY FOBS

This chapter focuses on finishing belts, hatbands, and key fobs. There will be referrals to other chapters for some of these steps. Since your first project should be a key fob, these directions are included first.

Supplies

- Metal or wood yardstick
- Ruler
- Pen
- Needle
- Strong thread
- Cutting blade (utility knife)
- Rubber mat, scrap wood, or something for a cutting surface
- Duco cement. This text references the use of Duco cement, which can be purchased at most variety stores. Any fast drying, clear glue may be substituted.
- Small scrap leather pieces
- Vise – optional

Finishing Key Fobs

Most key fobs are left in the round and not pressed. These directions are for finishing this kind of fob.

Three inches of hitching, plus a tassel at the bottom, makes a good key fob. They can be shorter or longer.

The tassel at the bottom will come from the dropped pulls, and the pulls brought down in the last row.

Cut a piece of soft leather ¼" wide and 4" long. This is for the metal key ring to slide over. The soft leather will be sewn on the end where the hitching was started (and opposite the tassel end).

Double the leather over, making it 2" long. Slip the raw ends into the middle of the key fob. Leave about a 1" loop sticking out. With needle and thread, sew the soft leather to the inside of the hitching. Make sure the leather is secure. Secure nylon string to the hitching with needle and thread. Clip excess string. Duco cement both the leather and the nylon string so they won't come undone. See Diagram #10-1

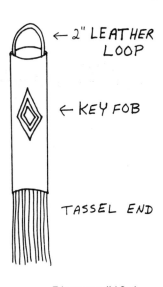

Diagram #10-1
Key Fob

On the tassel end, secure the nylon string with needle and thread. Clip off the excess string. Duco cement the area where the nylon string has been secured.

Make sure Duco cement is only used in areas where it will be covered with knots. It does *NOT* come off horsehair.

Cover both ends with knots. See Chapter 13, *Making Knots to Cover Joints*.

Add a metal key ring to the leather.

Trim the tassels. Comb the tassels out, using your fingers.

Tips

- If the pulls are too short to make good tassels, cut the pulls off, Duco cement, and cover the entire area with a knot.

- Some hitchers use horsehair instead of leather to hook the metal key ring on to. Leather is stronger than horsehair for this.

Finishing Belts

Pressing the Hitched Tube

Because hitching is worked over a dowel, a tube is formed as it is slipped off the dowel. When hitching is slipped completely off the dowel, you have a long tube. This tube has to be flattened to make a belt.

The hitched tube is put in a "press" to flatten it. A press is two pieces of half inch steel with nuts and bolts. The nuts and bolts are torqued down to apply pressure on the hitched tube and make it flat.

The word "press" is used in two ways. The two pieces of steel, with nuts and bolts, is called a press. It is also used as a verb, as in "press the belt".

Before proceeding further, go to Chapter 15, *The Horsehair Press*. Press your belt and then come back to this section for finishing the belt.

Measuring and Cutting the Finished Hitched Blank

Ideally, the actual hitched blank can be cut off on both ends to make the finished hitched blank. Chapter 9, *Sizing of Hitched Horsehair Items – Belts and Hatbands*, and Chapter 11, *How to Use Graph Paper*, cover this subject.

Now that the belt is out of the press, you should be able to see why both the first and last rows need to be cut off. The first row is a bit narrower in width. The last row has a hump and is wider.

Measuring for the finished hitched blank should be exact.

The following example illustrates cutting off the ends. The finished belt size is 32". The finished hitched blank should be 26".

The actual hitching done on the dowel was 27". However, the hitched blank came out of the press 26 ¾" long. One fourth inch was lost due to shrinkage. We're doing great – ¾" needs to be cut off the pressed blank to make it 26" long. Hitching that extra inch allowed for the shrinkage and cutting off both the first and last rows.

The same amount should be cut off both ends. If your tension and measurements remained consistent through the belt, the patterns should be the same distance from both ends. If you had a pattern in the middle of the hitching, the middle of that pattern should be the same distance from both ends of the blank.

Using the above example, $^3/_8$" needs to be cut off both ends of the belt ($^3/_8$" plus $^3/_8$" equals ¾").

Using the ruler, measure $^3/_8$" in from the end of the blank. Do this in two places. Draw a line with the pen. This is the cutting line.

Use a rubber mat or block of wood to cut on to protect the table surface.

Place the yardstick along the cutting line, using the yardstick for a cutting edge. Apply pressure with your hand to the yardstick so it won't slip. Cut along the cutting line with the utility knife. It usually takes more than one slicing to go through the hitched blank.

Rulers are easier to measure small amounts with. Yardsticks are easier to apply pressure on when cutting, especially metal yardsticks. Yardsticks are also necessary for accurate measurements of long items.

Remember, the measurements in this section are just an example. Your blank may only need ½" or $^5/_8$" cut off. Or even 1".

The finished hitched blank is now the exact measurement needed.

Gluing Both Ends of the Finished Hitched Blank

Duco cement is used to glue both ends of the finished hitched blank. This prevents unraveling when holes are put in the hitched blank to sew the leather ends on.

Duco goes only on the very ends of the hitched blank. It is difficult to remove and will be put only where it can be covered.

One end of the belt will be glued and allowed to dry. Then the other end will be glued.

Slightly open one end of the hitched blank and spread a small amount of Duco inside. On the outside, put a line of Duco all the way around the belt – front, back, and the cross hitch border. It spreads easily, so keep the Duco within $^1/_8$" of the end.

Put the hitched blank end in a vise to dry, first protecting it with a scrap of leather over the glued end. The vise applies pressure to the end, and presses the front and back together.

The leather scrap protects the hitched blank and prevents the glue from sticking to the vise. Wax paper can go between the leather and hitched blank.

When the glue is dry on one end, glue the other end.

The scrap leather will want to stick to the hitched blank so gently peel the leather off. If the glue was applied properly, the leather that sticks to the blank will be only in the area that will be covered up later with knots or leather.

Leather sticking to the blank may overlap the end of the hitched blank. Using the utility knife, cut the leather off flush with the hitched blank. Take care not to cut the hitched blank.

<u>Sewing the Hitched Blank to Leather Ends</u>

The belt is now ready for leather belt ends. Go to Chapter 12, *Leather Belt Ends*. There are many steps involved in finishing the belt, but it's all worth it when the belt is completed.

<u>Finishing Hatbands</u>

<u>General Information</u>

Hatbands can be finished with either leather ends or horsehair ends. Both ways require a 21" long finished hitched blank.

If the blank is pressed, cut and glue the hitched blank the same way the belt blank is done (see above).

If the blank is not pressed, hitch just a bit extra than 21" to take care of shrinkage when it comes off the dowel. Nothing will be cut off.

If the blank is hitched over rope, hitch exactly 21". Nothing will be cut off. The rope remains inside the hitched blank.

Directions for these 4 different hatbands follow.

<u>1. Hatbands with Pressed Hitched Blanks and Leather Ends</u>

These directions are based on a 25" brim circumference.

Reading the directions on hatband sizing in Chapter 9, *Sizing of Hitched Horsehair Items – Belts and Hatbands,* will help in understanding this section. Directions in Chapter 12, *Leather Belt Ends*, will also be needed.

Two inches of leather will be showing on each end. Therefore, there will be 2" from the hitched blank to the foldover where the buckle goes. There will be 2" from the hitched blank to the center hole on the tongue end. (There will be 3 holes in the tongue end, instead of the 5 holes which are on a belt.)

Cut 2 pieces of leather as wide as the pressed hitched blank. The tongue end will be 4 ½" long. The buckle end will be 3 ½" long. Finish per the directions in Chapter 12, *Leather Belt Ends*.

Sew leather ends to the finished hitched blank per directions in Chapter 12.

The foldover will have 2" showing on the topside; and approximately 1 ½" showing on the underside. Using the directions in Chapter 12, do the foldover, Chicago screws, 3 holes in the tongue billet end, and other finish work.

Cover the joint where the hitched blank and leather ends are sewn together. Do this with a thin strip of leather or knots. See Chapter 12, or Chapter 13, *Making Knots to Cover Joints,* for the appropriate directions.

2. Hatbands with Pressed Hitched Blanks and Horsehair Ends

Horsehair ends on hatbands are very attractive. These are called *tails*. Two tails will be needed. They are braided and are made of 4 pulls per braid (20 hairs per pull). Knots are commonly used to cover the joints where any sewing and gluing is done. See Photo #10-1 for a finished hatband with tails.

Making Pulls and Braiding the Tails

Pull 20 hairs for each pull. Usually the background color of the hitched blank is used for the tail color. Eight pulls are needed for 2 tails. The 4 pull braid makes a round braid.

Take 4 pulls and tie a string around one end of these 4 pulls. Loop the other string end over a hook. This holds the end while you are braiding.

Put 2 pulls in your left hand, and 2 pulls in your right hand. The pulls will probably naturally fall so one pull in each hand will look like it is on top. The other will look like it is on the bottom. If they do not naturally fall like this, then just pick one to be on the *top* and one on the *bottom.*

Take the top pull on your left, bring it behind all the other pulls, and over to the right side. Put it under the top right pull and over the bottom right pull. Bring it back to the left side. Now it will be on the bottom of the left side pulls.

Now go to the right side top pull, and do exactly what you did on the left.

Take the top pull on your right side, and go behind all the pulls. Go under the top left pull and over the bottom left pull. Bring it back to the bottom of your right side.

Continue doing this same thing. First take from the top left, then the top right. Braid down to the bottom end of the pulls. Tie a string at the bottom.

Make 2 of these round braids.

Double over one of the braids in half. One inch from the loop, wrap thread about 5 times around that spot. Knot the thread so it doesn't come off. Duco cement this area. This will be covered later with a knot. See Diagram #10-2.

Diagram #10-2
Braid Doubled Over and Loop Formed

Measure about 8 ½" from where the thread was wrapped by the loop. Also wrap this area with thread, going around all the horsehair. Duco cement this area, which will be covered later with a knot. The hairs sticking out from this end will be the tassels. See Diagram #10-3.

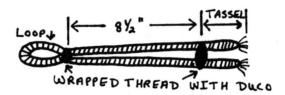

Diagram #10-3
Tail Wrapped with Thread and Duco Cement on Both Ends

Repeat these steps with the other 4 pull braid.

Attaching the Tails to the Hitched Blank

Sew the tails to the hitched blank with strong thread following these instructions.

Take the loop end of the 4 pull braid. Put it on top of the face of the hitched blank, as close to the end as possible. Where the tail is wrapped with string is the sewing area for attaching the tail to the hitched blank.

Using an awl, poke 2 holes in the pressed blank for a needle to go through. The tassel end will face away from the blank. See Diagram #10-4.

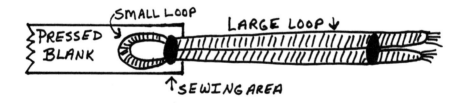

Diagram #10-4
Sewing Tails to the Hitched Blank

Securely sew the tail to the hitched blank. Make this area as small as possible. Tie the thread off. Duco cement the area. This will be covered with a knot.

Attach the other 4 pull braid in the same way to the other end of the hitched blank. See Chapter 13, *Making Knots to Cover Joints*. Use knots to cover the area where the tail has been sewn to the hitched blank.

Finishing the Tails

The tails just sewn on to the hitched blank circle around to finish forming the hatband.

Make a circle with the hatband. Take the right tail and put it through the large braided loop of the other tail. Continue taking it through the small loop formed over the hitched blank. The finished tassel area will lay over the hitching.

Take the left tail and put it through the small loop on the right side so the tassel area will lay over the hitched blank.

Here is where the size of the small loop is important. If the loop is too small, the tail won't go through. If the loop is too large, it looks out of balance with the hatband. As you make more hatbands, you will have a preference as to the size of your loops. These directions are just a guideline.

Slider Knot

The slider knot goes over all 4 braids of the tails. It allows the braids to slide back and forth. This makes the hatband larger or smaller.

This knot is **NOT** attached to the braids. Otherwise, it could not slide back and forth.

See Chapter 13, *Making Knots to Cover Joints*, for directions on slider knots.

Finishing the Tails

Knots cover the area on the end of the tail where thread has been wrapped. This area is where the tassel is. Before covering this area, determine if you want more hair in the tassels (also called fluffs). If so, go the next section. Come back to this section after adding more hair.

Cover this area with knots. See Chapter 13, *Making Knots to Cover Joints,* on how to make knots.

Cut the tassels the same length on both tails. The length is up to you. Fluff the hair by combing out the braid. Use your fingers to separate the individual hairs.

If the hairs are wildly sticking out, take twist ties and wrap around the tassels for a few days. Twist ties are the ties from the produce department at grocery stores. When shipping hatbands, put twist ties around the tassels to protect them.

Adding Extra Hair in the Tassels

Make a 4 pull braid. This is the same braid the tails are made of.

Double the braid over, making one side the length of the tassels, plus one inch.

Lay this doubled over braid on the tail where thread has already been wrapped around for the tassel. Wrap the new braid and old braid together in this same spot. Tie off the thread. Duco cement.

Never add tassels in any other way. If the hair is just laid in straight, it will come out. ALWAYS double over the added hair.

When putting extra hair on the tassel, wet the doubled over braid with water. It will lay down better.

Go back to the section on finishing the tails.

3. Hatbands in the Round with Horsehair Ends and
4. Hatbands Hitched Over Rope with Horsehair Ends

These hatbands take less preparation before sewing on the tails.

The nylon string on the first and last rows will have to be secured. If the string is long enough, thread a needle with the string. Pull the string into the middle of the hatband about an inch. Clip off the string. Or take regular fabric sewing thread, a small needle, and secure the string to the hitching. Clip off the string.

Duco cement the string.

Clip the excess part of the pulls off on the last row, flush to the hitched blank. Duco cement this area.

If hitching around a rope, clip the rope off, as flush to the hitched blank as possible. Sear the nylon rope with a match to keep the rope from unraveling. Be very careful and not burn the horsehair. Duco cement the rope and the pulls.

Go to the above section on making horsehair tails and attaching tails.

Chapter 11

HOW TO USE GRAPH PAPER

This chapter focuses on how to use graph paper to design patterns, advantages of using graph paper; when to use graph paper; understanding hitching so graph paper can be used; tips to make it easier to use graph paper; remedies or solutions when what is graphed isn't exactly what is wanted; and supplies needed.

Supplies

- Graph paper – 4 squares to the inch is ideal. Up to 32 face pulls can be graphed across the short end of the graph paper (enough for a 1 $^3/_8$" wide belt).
- Colored pens or pencils – for coloring the pattern lines on graph paper. Felt tip pens work better than pencils as they are quicker to draw with.
- Pencil – to draw your pattern on the graph paper. Fill in the pencil lines later with color.
- Eraser – self-explanatory!!! Yes, there will be those days when all the great pattern ideas in your head are hard to get down on paper.
- Scotch tape – for taping graph paper together end to end for patterns that are longer than one sheet.
- Scissors – for cutting graph paper off when just part of a sheet is needed to finish designing a pattern.
- Magnetic board – for reading the graph paper when hitching. The magnets serve 2 purposes: 1. Holding the graph paper to the metal board. 2. Marking the row you're working on. Magnetic boards can be found at fabric and craft stores.

Understanding Hitching so Graph Paper can be Used

Hitched rows are laid out like a brick wall. Bricks are not laid directly in line on top of each other. Each row in a brick wall is staggered so the wall is stronger. Hitched rows are the same way. See Diagram #11-1, then look at your own hitching to see the similarity.

Diagram #11-1
Hitched Rows Compared to a Brick Wall

Remembering which way an open hitch and closed hitch knot go is also crucial to understanding how to use graph paper.

A closed hitch knot drawn on paper goes to the left, and looks like this:

An open hitch knot drawn on paper goes to the right, and looks like this:

Using and understanding this information is the basis for using graph paper.

How to Use Graph Paper for Designing Patterns

Remember that hitching looks like a brick wall. Graph paper does not look like a brick wall. See Diagram #11-2.

Diagram #11-2
Comparisons Between Brick Walls, Hitching, and Graph Paper

Graph paper has to be altered for our purposes when designing hitching patterns. In open hitch rows, graph paper lines are used to mark the pattern. In closed hitch rows, put lines in the middle of each square when designing the pattern. This creates the brick wall effect. See Diagram #11-3.

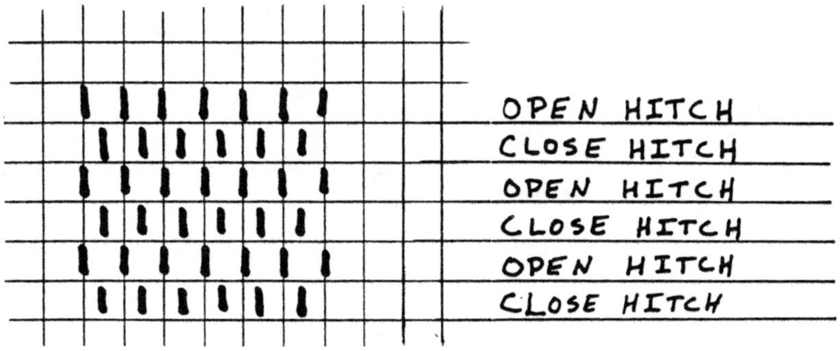

Diagram #11-3
Adapting Graph Paper for use in Designing Hitching Patterns

Without using graph paper, the diagram below shows what the very outside of a 6 row diamond looks like on paper. See Diagram #11-4. The arrows show what direction the outside pulls are going. From this diagram, figure out whether the knots are closed or open hitches. Use your 6 row diamond directions to help figure this out.

Diagram #11-4
6 Row Diamond on Paper

Diagram #11-5 shows which are open and which are closed hitch knots:

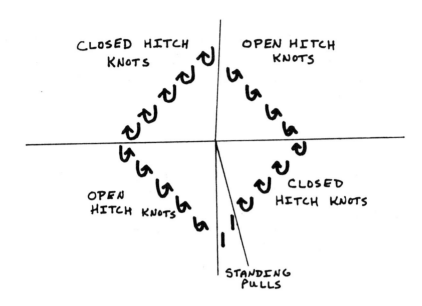

Diagram #11-5
6 Row Diamond on Paper with Open and Closed Knots, Standing Pulls

Knowing what direction on the graph paper that the pulls go, determines whether the knot should be a closed or open hitch knot. If the pattern goes toward the left, it's a closed hitch knot. If the pattern goes toward the right, it's an open hitch knot.

But what about the drop, add, and standing pulls? What determines how to know when to use this?

The term *reading graph paper* means looking at the pattern on graph paper. This indicates when to drop, add, stand, open hitch, or close hitch. It is literally *reading from left to right, top to bottom,* and knowing what to do with each colored line and background pull on the paper.

When reading graph paper, you will always be working with at least 3 rows. These are: the last row hitched, the row presently being hitched, and the next row to be hitched. Think of it as the past, present, and future.

Why do 3 rows have to be read when you're actually hitching only 1 row? Looking at the last row shows what was stood, and needs to be dropped in the present row. The present row shows whether the pulls are open hitched, closed hitched, dropped, added, or stood. The next row shows what needs to be added. Remember that each pull has to be done in sequence.

Knowing when to add: Look at the next row. What new colors are there? Add those new pulls in the present row, and hitch them in the next row.

Knowing when to stand a pull: Look at the present row. Which colors do not continue into the next row? Stand those pulls, and drop them in the next row.

Chapter 11: How to Use Graph Paper   73

<u>Knowing when to drop a pull:</u> Look at the last row. Are any of those pulls standing because they do not continue into the present row? If so, drop them in the present row.

<u>Knowing whether to open or close hitch a pull:</u> Study the graph paper and decide if the pull is to be dropped, added, or stood. If it is none of those three, then look at the next row and see which direction the colored line goes on the graph paper.

If it goes to the left, the pull is closed hitched.

If it goes to the right, the pull is open hitched.

Without using graph paper, Diagram #11-6 shows what the 6 row diamond looks like on paper. To conserve costs and make this book affordable to everyone, we use straight and wavy lines instead of color in this diagram. To make it easier to understand, color the pulls yourself, using the colors in Chapter 5, *How to Hitch a 6 Row Diamond*. Red is the very outside straight lines. Gold is the wavy lines. Blue is the middle straight lines.

Diagram #11-6
Complete 6 Row Diamond on Paper

Diagram #11-7 shows this same 6 row diamond graphed on graph paper. In open hitch rows, the pattern uses the regular graph paper lines. In closed hitch rows, the pattern lines are drawn in the middle of each square. This adapts the graph paper to the brick wall effect.

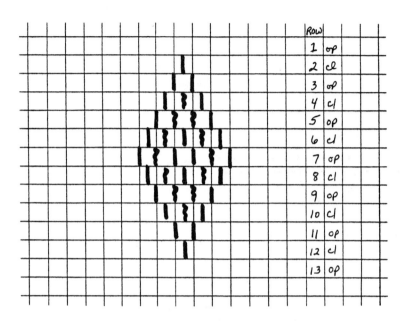

Diagram #11-7
6 Row Diamond on Graph Paper

Besides showing the graphed pattern of the 6 row diamond, Diagram #11-7 has other valuable information on it. Notice that each row is numbered, 1 through 13. You can always refer back to your directions if you're not sure what to do with the rows you're hitching.

Also notice that each row is marked as to whether it is open (op), or closed (cl). This tells if the background is open hitched or closed hitched. In graphing patterns, this information is crucial to knowing what to do with the background.

Get in the habit of numbering your rows, and marking if the background is open or closed hitch. This saves time down the road when you're actually hitching and reading the graph paper.

Two further questions remain. What is graphed? What happens to the background.

What is Graphed?

Graph only the background and pattern of the face pulls. Remember that the face pulls are the front of the belt, hatband, etc., where the pattern is. There is no need to graph the back of the belt, or the cross hitch border. Those pulls are always the same. Count the pulls in each row while hitching, but do not take the time to graph them out.

Only the face pulls (which includes both the background and pattern) are on the graph paper. The following chart gives the dowel size, number of face pulls, and finished width of the more common items.

Dowel Size	# of Face Pulls	Finished Width
$3/8$"	14	$3/4$"
$1/2$"	22	1"
$5/8$"	26	$1\ 1/4$"
$3/4$"	32	$1\ 3/8$"

What Happens to the Background?

To avoid confusion with the colored pattern, use other marks to show the background. Little *x's* work well. Mark the *x's* in the open hitch rows. An example shows this easier. Diagram #11-8 shows a 6 row diamond graphed out. We'll use a $3/8$" dowel for this example. There will be 14 face pulls.

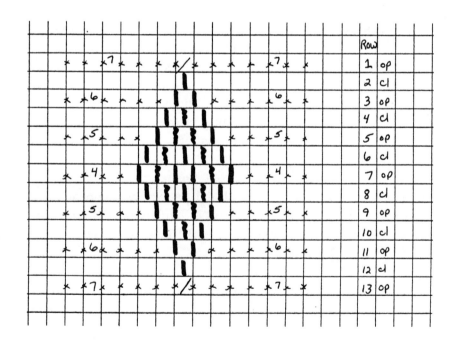

Diagram #11-8
6 Row Diamond with Pattern and Background Graphed

So why are the *x's* only put in the open hitch row and not in the closed hitch rows? There is rather an odd thing with the background in closed hitch rows. When going into a diamond, the closed hitch on the left side is in the same hole as the pattern (and is dropped in that row). This is difficult to graph.

When going out of a diamond, there are two background pulls in the same hole. One is closed hitched; the other is open hitched. This action lays the 2 pulls on top of each other so it looks like they are one pull. This is also difficult to graph.

This can be difficult to understand when first hitching. The count is supposed to be the same in each row. It takes time to grasp that the count looks the same in each row, but the actual pulls hitched is different. The *look* has to be there so the count will be the same in each row. One of the pulls is hidden by the other pull.

When reading graph paper for what to do with the background, look 2 rows ahead of the row being hitched. Remember that background pulls are added in open hitch rows when going out of a diamond. Therefore, you have to know whether or not to add background in an open hitch row so the background count will be correct in the next open hitch row.

Also, you have to know if you are going into a diamond, so appropriate steps are taken to drop the background pulls.

Refer to the Basic 6 Row Diamond directions as you use graph paper. Use these directions especially when figuring out what happens to the background. Remember, as hitching becomes more familiar, what to do with background pulls will become easier.

It may be easier for you to write directions down for a pattern before hitching. Include both the background and pattern pulls to familiarize yourself with how graph paper relates to actual hitching. We include patterns and examples in this book to get you started.

When first starting to learn, the colored pattern will appear to be the difficult part. Knowing what to do with the background is actually the difficult part. Using graph paper simplifies the pattern, no matter how difficult your pattern may look. The background can be the difficult part.

This is why the habit of numbering the rows and marking whether the background is open or closed hitch is important. It also speeds hitching to put down the number of background pulls in the open hitch row. You don't have to count *x's* when actually hitching. Diagram #11-8 shows this.

Slanted lines in the background help show when adding or dropping pulls. Notice in Diagram #11-8, Row 1: There are 7 *x's*; a slanted line; and 7 *x's*. This tells the hitcher to open hitch 7 background pulls; add a colored pattern pull; open hitch 7 background pulls. Fourteen background pulls are hitched, and the colored pattern pull has been added to go into the diamond.

Diagram #11-8, Row 13: This tells the hitcher to open hitch 7 background pulls; drop the colored pattern pull; open hitch 7 background pulls. Fourteen background pulls are hitched and the colored pull has been dropped to finish going out of the diamond.

What happens to the background pulls that are part of the pattern itself? Mark these with *x's* in both the open and closed hitch rows. With your knowledge of drop, add, stand, open, and close hitch, you will be able to figure out what to do with these background pulls.

Diagram #11-9 shows an example of this graphed out. Background pulls on either side of the pattern, and within the pattern are shown. Detailed directions for this pattern are in Chapter 20, *Complete Patterns and Directions*. This example is for a pattern with 22 face pulls (½" dowel).

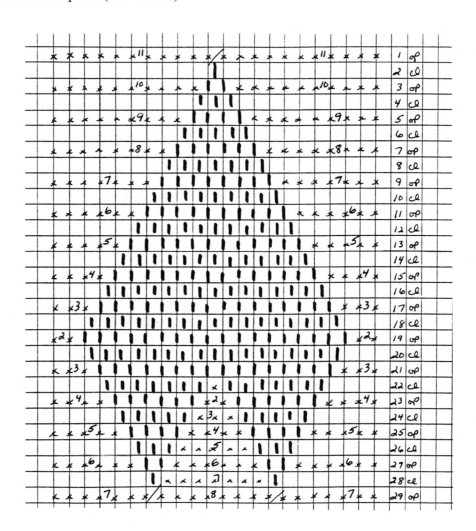

Diagram #11-9
Example of Background within a Graphed Pattern

Working with sample patterns in Chapter 20, *Complete Patterns and Directions,* will help in understanding what happens with the background.

Remember that in order to have straight rows instead of spiraling rows, the rows must be alternated with open and closed hitches. What is happening within the pattern will not create a spiral effect if the back, cross hitch border, and background face pulls are alternated with open and closed hitch rows. Your patterns can be as complex or simple as you wish.

Repetition in hitching is the only way to gain skill in hitching horsehair. Repetition in any aspect of your life is the best way to gain skill in those areas of your life that you want to be the best.

How to Use the Magnetic Board

The magnetic board should come with at least 2 magnetic strips. Three rows need to be showing: the last row hitched, the row presently being hitched, and the next row to be hitched (past, present, future). Put 1 magnetic strip right above the last row hitched. Put 1 magnetic strip right below the next row to be hitched. Three rows should be showing. The magnets hold the graph paper on the board.

Using Scotch Tape

Many patterns will be longer than 1 sheet of graph paper. Tape additional sheets of paper to each other with tape. Make sure the lines are lined up with each other. Tape on the backside.

Tips on Using Graph Paper

These tips are the little odds and ends that make a difference when using graph paper. Some are repeated elsewhere. Some will make no sense until you actually start working with graph paper and hitching from it.

- Always start and end the pattern on an open hitch row. This centers the pattern.

- Any apex of the pattern should be on an open hitch row. This centers the pattern, and the background comes out better.

- Read the graph paper from left to right, top to bottom.

- Read what happens to the pulls in consecutive order. Do what needs to be done with each pull in consecutive order. Otherwise your pattern will be off. This includes both the pattern pulls and the background pulls of the face.

- The actual hitched pattern over 2 strings of #9 nylon string looks longer than what the graph paper shows.

- When reading graph paper for background pulls, look 2 rows ahead of the row being hitched. Background pulls are added in open hitch rows. (See directions for rows 7-12 of the Basic 6 Row Diamond.)

- Use pencil lines to connect graphed lines before filling in with colored pens (like a dot-to-dot picture). Visualize what the inside of the pattern will look like. Make changes easily because pencil has been used.

- A pattern may be the exact same shape, but go different directions on the belt. This pattern requires two separate sets of directions and graphing. Example:

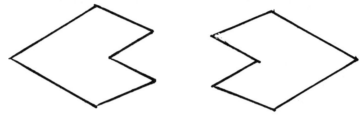

- Practice makes perfect.

Advantages of Using Graph Paper

The benefits of using graph paper make it worthwhile to learn. The largest benefit is in time saved while hitching. A project can also be laid out entirely on paper so your sizing of the hitched blank can be more accurate.

Experimenting with patterns is one thing that makes hitching so interesting. A wide variety of patterns makes items more salable, shows the skills of a good hitcher, and takes hitching from being merely functional to an art form.

Graph paper provides this vast array of patterns without going through the costly use of time in hitching to figure out something new.

By not using graph paper, mistakes take longer to catch. Time is lost in taking out the hitching and redoing it so the pattern comes out right.

It is said that a good hitcher can hitch one inch per hour. This varies with the width of the item, and the complexity of the pattern.

Yes, it does take time to figure out a pattern on paper, and what colors go where. But it is more frustrating and time consuming to take out mistakes in the actual hitching. Take advantage of every available tool to enjoy hitching. Graph paper is one of these tools.

Sometimes there will be a pattern in your head that is just saying "*Hitch me, Hitch me*". Laying this pattern out on paper first saves time when experimenting with something new. Maybe this "Hitch me, Hitch me" pattern will look real yucky if it's actually done. Or maybe it's a real breakthrough pattern that is wonderful, and your mind expands on it further. Laying it out on paper first gives an indication of this.

Using graph paper also gives more accurate measurements even before starting a project. This alleviates guesswork when figuring out the actual hitched blank that is needed for a project.

A project can be laid out entirely on paper before hitching is even begun. The following example of a belt shows how this works. Assume a custom order for a 32" belt size. Subtract 6" for belt ends, which means the finished hitched blank needs to be 26" long.

One inch is added due to:
1. Shrinkage when the blank is pulled off the dowel
2. Variations in estimates
3. Cutting off the first and last rows

Therefore, figure on hitching 27".

Estimate the actual completed inches of the pattern. To do this, divide the number of rows in the graphed pattern by how many rows per inch you hitch.

Example: There are 48 rows in the graphed pattern. You hitch 8 rows per inch. Divide 48 by 8 which equals 6. Therefore, the completed pattern should be 6" long. Call this Pattern A.

Pattern B has 33 rows. It's estimated completed length will be 4". (33 divided by 8 equals 4 $^1/_8$").

To lay the hitched blank out on paper, the following information is needed:

The length of background wanted on both ends.
The patterns desired for the belt, and the estimated length of each.
The length of the finished hitched blank.
The length that will actually be hitched.

Using the above information, lay the belt out like this (Bgrd means background color):

3"	6"	2 ½"	4"	2 ½"	6"	3"
Bgrd	Pattern A	Bgrd	Pattern B	Bgrd	Pattern A	Bgrd

The totals of the estimated background, Pattern A, and Pattern B, add up to 27", which is the actual hitched length that is wanted in this example. Remember to use a wood or metal ruler when measuring the actual hitching. Cloth measuring tapes can stretch.

Any project can be laid out like this. The benefit to doing this is that there is little guesswork as to the length of the finished project. A custom order should turn out exactly the length that is wanted.

The background lengths can be whatever and wherever you want, as long as the total of the hitched blank adds up to what is required. The above description is just an example.

Sometimes, though, the actual hitched length is not the same as the estimated length. Why does this happen? There are several reasons why.

As a hitcher becomes more experienced, the hitching becomes tighter and the rows per inch increases. The hitcher may be figuring that he is hitching 8 rows per inch, but actually is now hitching 9 ½ rows per inch.

Estimates on the pattern length are just that – estimates only. The estimate may have been rounded off higher. When rounding off, go with the conservative lower estimate. Especially when fractions of an inch are used, the estimate can be off from what is actually hitched.

Patterns are started on an open hitch row. The actual measuring may be off a row due to this. So there may not be the exact amount of background needed according to how the belt is laid out on paper.

These are all good reasons on why to hitch one inch extra than the finished blank. The one inch helps take up the slack.

Remedies/Solutions With Using Graph Paper

If the estimates are longer than what is actually hitched, the finished blank may end up shorter than what is expected. Following are remedies/solutions for this.

1. Add more rows of background somewhere in the belt. Make sure equal amounts are added so the belt is balanced.

2. Change a pattern mid-stream, and add more rows. This is more time consuming than adding rows of background, but it can be done. There are 2 ways of doing this.

a. If hitching has not been started on the pattern, add new rows on both ends of the pattern.

b. Add new rows in the middle of the pattern. Cut graph paper down the pattern middle. Add extra rows. Tape it back together.

3. Take a longer pattern and replace it for the shorter pattern. Using the above belt example, replace Pattern #B with Pattern #C.

One of my first custom orders I had this problem. The belt was laid out on paper. I thought everything was great. I got to the middle of the belt and knew I would be short at least 1". I used solution 2b to solve this dilemna. It was the good/bad. I had made that crossover to hitching tighter. It made for a better belt, but threw me for a loop till I figured out what had happened and how to solve the situation.

NEVER, EVER stretch the finished hitched blank to make it longer. It won't stretch enough to compensate for the needed extra length; and it can damage the hitched rows.

Periodically measure how many rows per inch you hitch. This will change as you become more skilled in hitching. Being consistent in your hitching tension is more important than how many rows per inch are hitched. Eight - 8 ½ rows per inch is fine. The more rows per inch that are hitched, the more time consuming the project.

The actual hitched blank may be longer than what is estimated. This is not a problem. To get the length you want, either cut off more (equally) on both ends. Or, make a belt for a larger belt size if this is not a custom order.

When to Use Graph Paper

Pictorials are more advanced designs. Learning to use graph paper will help you in designing these patterns.

Use it for everything!!!

Tip

- Think of patterns in terms of diamonds, or partial diamonds. Instead of looking at the whole pattern, start breaking it down into parts and find where the whole diamonds are. The pattern will start to look simpler in terms of hitching it.

Chapter 12

LEATHER BELT ENDS

This chapter focuses on making leather belt ends; suppliers of leather and leather tools; measurements and sizing; attaching the hitched blank to leather ends; and necessary supplies/tools/materials.

There are several ways to make leather ends and sew the leather to the hitched horsehair blank. Leather belt ends are also called billets. The basic directions for working with leather are the same. The difference is in how the leather and hitched blank are actually joined. It would be to your advantage to read through this chapter first. Then decide how your leather ends should be joined to the hitched blank before actually starting to measure and cut. Both ways have advantages.

Suppliers of Leather and Leather Tools

The appendix at the back of this book lists suppliers of leather and leather tools.

Some suppliers sell ready made belts that can be cut and attached to the hitched blank. Others sell belt ends or belt blanks that may need tooling or dyeing to finish the leather before attaching to the hitched horsehair blank.

There are plenty of books and suppliers that provide detailed information on leatherwork. We believe leatherwork is an art in itself. In this book, we provide a minimum of information for making belt ends. For more extensive information, and how to tool and carve leather, contact the list of suppliers, bookstores, adult education programs, and stores that carry leatherwork products.

Supplies

- Leather, 2-3 oz.; 4-5 oz.; 8-9 oz. (depending on your preference)
- Yardstick, metal or wood
- Cutting blade (utility knife)
- Awl
- Skiver
- Groover or Edge creaser
- Strap end punch

- #3 Beveler (also called edger)
- Rotary Punch or Mini punch set
- Mallet
- Oblong punch
- Rubber mat (for cutting on)
- Small piece of scrap wood (for cutting or pounding on)
- Beeswax
- Barge cement, or alternative glue. Some stores sell Barge only to wholesale companies for industrial use. Barge is prohibited in most prisons, so an alternative glue is needed. Check with your leather supplier for the best alternative to Barge.
- Duco cement
- Edge kote dye
- Leather dye
- Q-tips
- Strong thread
- Harness needle (blunt end), size 1/0 or 3/0
- Small piece of canvas
- Acrylic resolene
- Chicago screws, ¼" long; or Snap fasteners

Leather Needed

Leather comes in various thicknesses (also called weight). The best weight for belt ends is 8 to 9 ounce leather. Leather can be glued together to get the proper thickness. For instance, glue 2 pieces of 4 ounce leather together. Or, glue 1 piece of 3 ounce leather to 1 piece of 5 ounce leather.

The finish on your leather also makes a difference. Do you plan on tooling or carving on it? If so, the leather must be vegetable tanned so it can be wetted and the proper tools used on it.

Do you plan on using leather that is already finished? These leathers are usually thinner (2 to 3 ounces), and need to be glued to heavier ounce leather for stability. Using these leathers is less time-consuming, and give a dressier look to the belt. This is the option we use, unless the customer wants tooled leather ends.

Gluing Leather Thicknesses Together

If you are working with just 1 thickness of leather, skip this section.

As mentioned above, several thicknesses of leather may be glued together to get the desired thickness. The finished weight of 8 ounce leather is most desirable for belt ends. Any combination of weights of leather can meet this.

Glue together larger pieces than necessary for one project. Exact leather measurements will be cut from the larger leather as needed.

Use Barge Cement to glue the leathers together. This is a strong, durable cement. Barge must be used on both pieces that are glued together. Brush Barge on the backs of both pieces. ***DO NOT*** immediately place both pieces together. ***WAIT!!!*** Barge cement holds best when the glue is tacky and barely sticks to your fingers if you touch it. When the Barge has reached this point, place both leather pieces together. Carefully smooth the leather, pressing firmly, so there will be no air pockets.

Measuring for Leather Ends

The width of your hitched blank determines the width of the leather. Hitchers use the widths of 1", 1 ¼", and 1 ⅜" wide belts.

Sometimes these widths are approximate, and the hitched blank may be $1/16$" or $1/8$" wider or narrower. Each end of the same hitched blank can be different widths.

Determine the width that you want to use. Remember that the hitched blank and the leather belt ends have to both look good to have a high-quality belt.

We use the following cut lengths for belt ends:

6" – length of foldover end (where the buckle is attached).

8 ½" – length of end where the holes are punched for the buckle to hook into (called tongue end).

Belt ends can be longer. We feel these measurements give a good balance between the hitched blank and leather.

Cutting Leather Ends

On one long side of the leather, make sure the edge is straight. If it is not, cut it straight with the utility knife and a yardstick (preferably metal). To protect the table surface, use a rubber mat, or some kind of cutting board, under the leather.

Measure the width of the leather ends and mark with the utility knife. Marking with the knife is more accurate than a pen. Line up the yardstick with the 2 marks. Cut down the edge with the knife.

Cut 2 lengths of leather. One will be 6" long. One will be 8 ½" long.

On the 6" Long Piece of Leather

Using the skiver, skive the underside of one end about ¾" back from the end. Skiving shaves off some of the leather so it isn't as thick and lays down better when the leather is folded over for the buckle.

Using either the stitching groover or the edge creaser, groove approximately $3/16$" in from the long edge of both sides. This marks where the machine stitching or saddle stitching goes. **DO NOT** groove either the skived short end, or the other short end. The unskived short end is where the leather and hitched blank will be sewn together.

On the 8 ½" Long Piece of Leather

Using the strap end punch and a mallet, cut off one end of the leather to create a rounded edge. Make sure the punch is equal distance from both sides. Use a piece of wood or rubber mat for the hammering surface. The wood protects the other cutting surfaces.

Using the stitching groover or edge creaser, groove the leather front on both long sides and the curved end. **DO NOT** groove the straight short end. The straight end is where the leather and hitched blank will be sewn together.

Finishing both the 6" and 8 ½" Long Leather Ends

The rest of these directions apply to both billets.

Using a #3 edge beveler, round off the edges of both pieces of leather. Edge both the front and back of the leather. Do not edge the short end where the leather is sewn to the hitched blank. The edger takes the sharp edges off the leather. Do not edge finished lighter weight leather if it is used on the top side.

Take 80 grit sandpaper and rub the rough edging off. Then change to 220 grit sandpaper to sand the rough edging off.

Tooling and stamping must be done before dye is applied. Do this step now if your belt ends will be tooled.

Dyeing leather: If the front of the leather is to be dyed, use the chosen color. Follow directions on the bottle.

Edge Kote dye: Edge Kote is dye put on the edge of the leather. Use the appropriate color to match the leather front color. Use Q-tips to put it on. Edge carefully so dye is even where the edge meets the leather backside. Two coats of Edge Kote looks best.

Sewing in the groove: Using either a leather sewing machine or hand saddle stitching, sew in the groove made with the groover or edge creaser. Leave a bit of thread on both sides. Sear the thread with a match. This melts the nylon thread so there is no need for knotting or backstitching. Sewing finishes off the leather edges. It also strengthens leather if 2 pieces are glued together.

Refer to leather books for directions on saddle stitching.

Using beeswax: Beeswax and friction on the edge of the leather smooth the edge. Rub beeswax down the edge of the leather. Take a small piece of canvas, and rub rapidly up and down the edge. Friction creates heat, which softens the beeswax, and smoothes the edge. This may have to be repeated numerous times.

Sewing Belt Ends to Hitched Horsehair Blank

The leather belt ends (billets) are literally sewn to the hitched horsehair blank.

Use a size 1/0 harness needle. Thread the needle with strong thread, doubled over. Knot on the end. Run the thread through beeswax to prevent fraying.

Use an awl to poke 5 holes in the 1 $3/8$" wide leather billets; 4 holes in the 1 $1/4$" and 1" wide leather billets. Put a piece of wood under the leather to protect the table surface. Poke the first and last holes in the groove part. Make sure you do *NOT* poke the scived end of the 6" piece of leather. The holes should be evenly spaced. Poking from both the front and back makes the hole larger, and the needle goes through easier.

See Chapter 10, *Finishing Belts, Hatbands, and Keyfobs.* The hitched blank needs to be finished properly before doing the next steps.

Poke holes in the hitched blank with the awl. Holes should be past the first row of hitching so it holds better. The awl should go through the hitched blank where Duco cement was put. Space the holes so they will be directly across the holes punched in the leather.

Start on one side, drawing the needle up through the leather, and down through the hitched blank. Do this several times on the edge to make it stronger. Cross over to the next holes. Making *XXXX's* works best for sewing the middle holes together. Go through the holes several times, back and forth between the leather and hitching. Work over to the other edge. Sew the other edge together in one straight line. Do this several times. The leather edges should be lined up with the hitched edges. See Diagram #12-1.

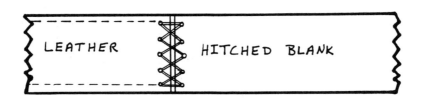

Diagram #12-1
Sewing Leather Ends to Hitched Blank

Work the thread back over to the starting side, putting it through the leather at the end.

Covering the Joint where Leather and Hitching have been Sewn Together.

The joint where leather ends and the hitched blank have been sewn together has to be covered. This joint can be covered with knots or leather. See Chapter 13, *Making Knots to Cover Joints*, if you choose to use knots.

If covering with leather, use 2-3 ounce leather the same color as the leather ends. Cut the leather $^5/_8$" wide. This is called the cover strip. Skive the back of both long edges so it lays down better. To obtain the necessary length of the cover strip, wrap leather around the joint, plus add $^3/_8$". Cut 2 lengths. To make the ends lay down flat, skive the underside of one end; and skive the topside of the other end. The skiving is important because these ends will be folded over each other.

Barge cement is used to glue the cover strip to the belt. Barge cement the skived part on the topside of the leather cover strip. Barge cement the entire underside of the leather cover strip. Make sure the leather is coated well with Barge.

Barge around the joint, on both the leather and hitched blank where they are sewn together. Be careful so the Barge is not wider than $^5/_8$" on this area. Make sure the sides of the hitched blank and leather are covered with Barge. Barge will rub off on finished leather. It will not rub off on rough leather or the hitched blank.

Remember, Barge holds better if it sets up and is tacky before the two pieces are glued together. This is because of glue tension. Be patient before placing the cover strip on.

The seam of the cover strip will be on the underside of the belt. Lay the cover strip over the joint, starting from the back of the belt. Work it around on the belt. Press firmly on all parts, making sure to get air bubbles out. Let it dry.

Alternative to Covering the Joint with Knots or a Cover Strip

Leather billets can be machine sewn or saddle stitched over the area where the hitched blank meets the leather. The hitched blank will be sandwiched between 2 pieces of leather. The hitched blank still needs to be cut and finished with Duco. See Chapter 10, *Finishing Belts, Hatbands, and Key Fobs.*

The leather sewn over the hitched blank can have a decorative curve to it instead of being squared off. See Diagram #12-2.

Diagram #12-2
Hitched Blank Sandwiched Between Leather

The disadvantage to using this method is that there is more bulk due to 3 layers sewn together – 2 layers of leather, and the hitched blank. Sewing and gluing must be carefully done, with no raw edges of hitching showing. Otherwise, the hitching could unravel.

Chicago Screws and Fold Over on 6" Leather Billet

The foldover on this end is where the belt buckle is attached. Measure 3 $\frac{1}{8}$" up from the joint where the hitched blank and leather are sewn together. Since this joint is covered, this will be an approximation.

On the leather underside, wet this area with water. When leather is folded over, water is applied so the leather won't crack. Fold the leather over, with the undersides together.

Use Chicago screws that are ¼" long. Mark where the holes go with the awl. These are punched with the rotary punch. The first hole is punched 1 $\frac{1}{8}$" in from the backside of the foldover. The second hole is punched 1" from the first hole. Both holes are centered in the billet.

A Mini punch set and mallet can be used. Use size 5 ($\frac{11}{64}$") in the mini punch set for Chicago screw holes. Mini punch sets are easier to use than rotary punches.

Using a screwdriver, secure the Chicago screws in the holes in the billet.

A leather or metal keeper goes between the 2 Chicago screws. See below for directions for making keepers. Keepers keep the tongue end from flopping around.

If using snaps, apply per manufacturer's directions.

Finishing the 8" Leather Billet

Five holes are punched in the 8" leather billet. These holes are where the buckle hooks in. The middle hole is the center hole discussed throughout this book. This billet is also called the tongue end.

To determine where these holes are punched, measure 3" from where the hitched blank and leather are joined. This is an approximation since this area is covered. Mark this with an awl. Use the size of the rotary punch which matches the buckle prong to make this hole. This is the center hole. Use a yardstick to measure from the foldover of the leather end to the center hole to make sure the belt size is accurate.

The other holes are spaced ¾" from each other, on either side of the center hole. See Diagram #12-3. If you are using a Mini punch set, use size 3 ($^9/_{64}$") for the holes.

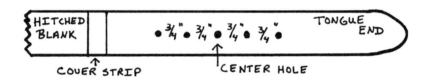

Diagram #12-3
Center Hole and Other Holes on 8" Billet (Tongue End)

THE MEASUREMENT FROM THE FOLDOVER TO THE CENTER HOLE IS THE BELT SIZE OF THE BELT. This measurement uses a standard 1 ½" length belt buckle.

For a protective leather coating, put Acrylic Resolene on the leather underside. Leather stores may recommend other products for this same purpose.

Making Keepers

Keepers should be the same color leather as the billets. Good widths for keepers are $^3/_8$" for wider belts, and ¼" for narrower belts. Lengths are determined by wrapping the keeper leather around the area where the keeper goes with both billets included in this measurement. Mark the place to cut with the utility knife. Add just a smidgen in length so the billet is easy to pull through the keeper.

It is easiest to prepare a longer piece of keeper leather and cut it off as needed. Short, narrow pieces of leather are harder to make. Also, it is more time efficient to already have the keeper leather done.

Edge the keeper sizes with the #3 Beveler. Edge Kote with the appropriate color. Smooth the edge with beeswax and canvas.

On the narrower keeper, poke a hole with the awl on each end of the keeper. Sew together with the same thread used in sewing the hitched blank and leather billets together.

On the wider keeper, poke 2 holes on each end. Sew together with an *X*. Sear the thread with a match.

Put water on the inside of the keeper to prevent the leather from cracking. Position the leather between the two Chicago screws, with the sewn part hidden by the billet. Run the tongue end of the leather through the keeper. Let the keeper dry so it is formed to the belt.

Oblong Punch

Depending on the type of belt buckle used, a slot hole may have to be punched in the foldover billet end. A ¾" oblong punch is a good size. The hole is punched where the fold is to allow the buckle through the hole.

Lay the billet end flat. Place the oblong punch centered from the edges, and equal distance on either side where the fold is. Use the mallet to hammer the punch, with a piece of wood underneath to protect the table surface. See Diagram #12-4.

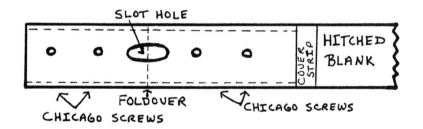

Diagram #12-4
Oblong Punch in Foldover Billet End

Odds and Ends

Sharpen the leather tools periodically.

These same general directions apply to leather ends on headstalls and hatbands. The leather measurements will be different for these other projects.

Horsehide (2-3 ounce) works great for cover strips as it stretches well and is durable.

Another option for billets is to locate a saddlemaker, shoe repair place, or leather worker to make billets for you.

Chapter 13

MAKING KNOTS TO COVER JOINTS

This chapter focuses on making knots with either thread or horsehair pulls to cover joints.

General Information

Knots cover areas where items are sewn or glued. This includes key fob ends and joints where leather and hitched work is sewn together. Knots are decorative as well as functional.

A knot is the entire covered area using this traditional method. Knot also refers to each individual step that is done to form the entire finished knot. This can be confusing to the beginner. Knots are sometimes called buttons.

Knotting with thread is easier than using horsehair. A well done knot with thread is more acceptable than a poorly made horsehair knot. The method of knotting is the same, whether using thread or horsehair. Saddle stitching thread works well, and wears better than a horsehair knot.

Supplies

- String/Thread same diameter as a 10 hair pull, such as
    Saddle stitching thread
    Waxed linen thread
    Artificial sinew
- Beeswax – for unwaxed thread
- Harness needle – blunt point, 1/0 or 3/0

Knotting a Key Fob with Waxed Thread

General Information

Knots cover both ends of the key fob, the beginning and ending hitched rows, and Duco cement area.

Use waxed string the same diameter as a 10 hair pull. Saddle stitching thread works well. Wax the thread with beeswax if it is not waxed to prevent fraying and tangling.

A base for the knot first needs to be made with the thread. The first row of actual knotting catches pulls from the key fob to keep the knot from sliding around.

Diagrams are loosely drawn. In reality, the thread is drawn up tight.

Making the Base

Cut about 30" of thread. Thread the needle with 3" of thread through the needle eye. Knot the bottom of the long end. Put the needle through a pull on the side of the key fob, approximately ¼" from the end. Pull till the knot is against the key fob.

Wrap the thread all the way around the key fob. Bring the needle up through the loop just formed, and pull tight. This is the base. See Diagram #13-1.

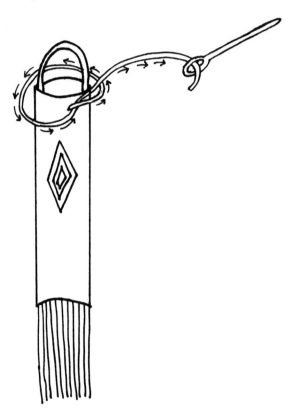

Diagram #13-1
Forming the Base of the Knot

First Row of Knotting

Put the needle under the base, catching one of the pulls on the key fob. Have the thread on the backside of your needle. Bring the needle up and pull all the way through.

Headstall with leather ends by Shoni.

Klein bridle with reins.

Belt pattern by Shoni.

Checkbook cover with hitched inlay.

Old Rawlins, WY bridle, with matching reins by Shoni.

Margolis headstall.

Pattern by Shoni, adapted from an old Blackfeet Indian mountain design.

Old headstall, restored by Shoni.

Belts by Shoni; silverwork by Ron Maulding. Copyright © 1996, Shoni Maulding, Double Eagle and Eagle designs.

Baw's Cane by Shoni, with sterling silver banding by Ron Maulding.

Belt patterns.

Kimball headstall with matching reins by Shoni.

Necklace with hitched horsehair.

Sterling silver banding on belt by Ron Maulding.

If the thread does not naturally fall on the needle backside, take your fingers and put it there. You will be working from left to right. Make sure pulls are picked up with the needle, as this prevents the knot from sliding around. See Diagram #13-2

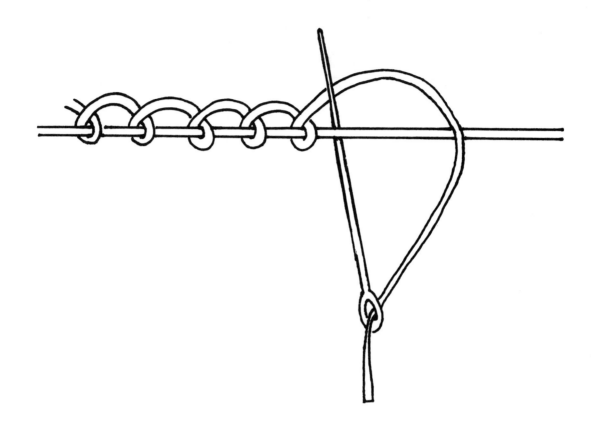

Diagram #13-2
Knotting First Row

After doing this a few times, you should be able to see *eyes*.

The first row is the only time hair is picked up from the key fob. When you have completed your first row, look for the *eyes*. The eye is where the needle goes through from now on. See Diagram #13-3

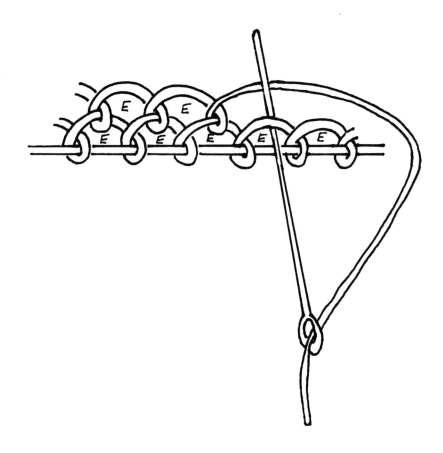

Diagram #13-3
Eyes in Knots

Continue sewing through the eyes till the area is covered.

When finished knotting, run the thread through the inside of the knot. Bring the needle out from under the entire knot. Clip off excess thread.

Increasing and Decreasing

When the area knotted becomes smaller, decrease by skipping an eye and going through the next one.

If the area becomes larger, increase by going through the same eye twice. The next row will have 2 eyes instead of one in that spot.

Adding New Thread, If Necessary

It may take more thread to cover the area. Add new thread by taking the needle and going straight down under the last eye which has been knotted. Bring the needle out from under the entire knot. This secures what has been knotted.

Rethread the needle. Go under and up the entire knot, bringing the new thread up behind the last eye that was knotted. Bring the new thread through the backside of this last eye that was knotted. Go over to the next eye, and continue knotting.

Continue knotting until the whole area is covered. When done, bring the needle under the entire knot to finish off. Clip off excess thread.

Both ends of the new thread should be under the knot, so nothing should unravel.

Knotting with Horsehair Pulls

Knots are made with the same pulls hitching is done with. It is easier to knot with wet hair. Put 6 pulls, color of your choice, in warm water about 15 minutes.

Take one pull. On one end, cut off the knot and thread the needle with the pull. Trim the hairs sticking out from the knot on the other end. Do not cut the knot off.

Follow the directions above for knotting.

When finished, trim any loose hairs so the knot will be smooth.

Tips

- Keep the horsehair pull wet while knotting. Wet hair lays down better.

- If possible, figure out which end of the pull was twisted first when pulling hair. Use that end to thread the needle as the twisting can make a difference with how the hair lays down.

Knotting Pressed Hitching

Needles can not go through pressed hitching to secure the knot to the hitching. Use thread to prepare a base for the knot to hook into, both at the beginning and end of the knotted area. The base will be on both the hitched blank and leather.

Thread used for knots can be used for this base. The same holes used in sewing the hitched blank and leather together can be used for the base. Make the base on the frontside and backside.

Catch the base string when beginning and ending the knot. Make sure the base string is covered with knots so it does not show.

Slider Knots

Slider knots are **NOT** attached to hitching or braiding. This allows them to do what the name says – slide up and down whatever it is knotted over.

Slider knots are made exactly the same as regular knots, except for *do not catch any hair with the needle.*

Slider knots can be knotted over a small piece of leather. The leather is sewn around the hitched item, but is not sewn to the hitching. The leather has to freely slide also.

Slider knots are commonly used on hatbands with braided horsehair tails, and bridles or headstalls.

Hitched Knots

Joints can also be covered with hitched knots.

Artificial sinew can be used. To dye artificial sinew, put in very hot water to get the wax out, or it will not dye. Dye the sinew. More than one dye bath may be necessary for the desired color. Wax with beeswax. Dyeing artificial sinew is time consuming.

Chapter 14

CHOOSING COLORS AND PATTERNS

This chapter focuses on choosing colors and patterns. What are sources of color combinations? How are patterns chosen? How are colors and patterns brought together in harmony?

Choosing Colors

Determining colors in patterns and backgrounds awakens the creative mind.

A color harmony wheel, bought at any art supply store, shows complementary colors.

Your own personal preferences will show in your work. This is where customers' color preferences are good. It will stretch your brain to use colors you ordinarily wouldn't work with.

Nature provides a wonderful source of color combinations. Take a walk and look at pansies, irises, or wildflowers. The combinations are wild. The colors are bright, almost neon like; or subtle and pastel. Green in nature is a vast array.

Sunrises and sunsets have colors that would look totally unnatural if painted on canvas. But up in the sky, it's spectacular.

I once had a customer who liked the high quality of my products, but the colors were too electric for him. He wanted something with more natural colors. That very week I found the tiniest flower on a long stalk. The petals were a vivid neon pink. Look around, see what nature is. I dare you to explore color.

Okay, so both you and your customers like things more subtle. Look at your surroundings again. Maybe you're in rocky areas where colors can be more subtle. Or it's late August in the prairies, and there's been a drought. Everything is just whispers of brilliancy.

Or you're in a foggy city in the dead of winter. Or a prison environment. Look around again. See what your environment is. Again, I dare you to explore color.

So you dislike walking, hate flowers (you're allergic to pollen), or are behind bars. That's no excuse. There are plenty of books and magazines in libraries. Order gardening catalogs and look at the pictures.

You say you like to shop?? Try out the color combinations at clothing stores. Or how about fabric stores... People browse at fabric stores for hours. You can too – looking at colors.

Try out the safe color combinations. Then stretch your mind.

Or, try very simple combinations – perhaps red, black, and white on a black background. That's simple enough. But instead of making the item blah, make it *WOW* by the choice of patterns and how the colors are arranged in that pattern.

Remember that what is wow to me, may be blah to you. So again, stretch your imagination. Let inspiration guide you. Do a variety of color combinations.

Tip

- A little bit of orange or yellow goes a long way. Our bias is against orange, so I have no problem using very little, or none, of this. Unless a customer wants a predominantly orange or yellow item, use these two colors sparingly.

Choosing Patterns for Colors

Most any pattern can be used with any color combination.

If there is little contrast between the colors, place several rows of the same color side by side. For example, 2 rows of white, next to 2 rows of light blue, next to 2 rows of light lilac. The colors will then stand out instead of blending into each other.

Sometimes a customer will like a particular pattern, but pick totally different colors. Hitch the same pattern shape. Then carefully choose how those other colors will be placed in the pattern. The inside of the pattern may be completely changed. This is one example of how great it is to use graph paper.

Take individual colored pulls and hold them next to each other. Does it look good? Also hold those pulls against the background color. Can the colored pulls be seen? Do you want them to be seen?

Choosing Patterns

We strongly suggest learning how to use graph paper. This will expand your patterns. You will also quickly develop more intricate patterns.

Most patterns are based on diamonds, which is why the 6 row diamond is the first pattern learned.

There are some things that cannot be hitched perfectly because of the very nature of how hitched rows lay. Circles are one example.

Inspiration, quiet time, and a blank piece of graph paper and pencil are great for starters in creating patterns. If you get an idea while on the go, sketch it out, and later transfer the idea to graph paper.

Some geometric Indian beadwork patterns can be converted to hitching patterns. Again, spend time at the library.

Tips

- This is your chance to choose. Reach for the sky.

BAW'S CANE

I always called my paternal grandfather "Baw". As I grew into early adulthood, this became a source of embarrassment for me, so I referred to him as my grandfather to outsiders. The name, Baw, stuck; even to his graveside at age 94 where it was put on the flowers.

He was a tough, old Swede, called a character by the Valley people. His parents came over on the boat, and met in Montana. Baw bought a ranch in western Montana in 1926, the one I grew up on. He was a workaholic, expecting much from drifters asking for room and board in exchange for work. I always thought he'd die in an irrigation ditch.

I remember his kerosene lantern bobbing down the driveway at night when he was going out to check the cattle at calving time. He liked to talk, but not listen. Anyone around him was in for a dissertation.

Baw's cane has been fancied up a bit. The flags symbolize the family coming to America, and the son who survived Pearl Harbor. Baw's birth and death years are hitched. The middle pattern is a traditional Blackfoot Indian beadwork "mountain" pattern. The rest is just because I like bright colors. Sterling silver banding completes both ends.

We didn't do anything with the handle. I wanted it to retain the feel of an old man's rough, calloused hands that smoothed the wood – the tough, old Swede I called Baw.

Bev Klein's Headstall

This horsehair hitched bridle came into my possession after my father died in 1934. It had been pawned to him in Kellogg, Idaho, probably in the 1920's. The person who pawned it told him it was hitched in Deer Lodge, Montana, at the prison. It was only recently that I began trying to authenticate its maker.

A sculpture friend who saw this piece felt sure it was the work of a Native American acquaintance of his from his youth. I made two trips to Browning, Montana, to the Museum of the Plains Indians to further my research. There I found the name of the hitcher's son who is an artist. After tracking him to Fort Belnap, Montana, I was able to correspond with him, sending several pictures of the bridle. He is sure this piece is one of his father's.

The dowel is wrapped with brain tanned leather, then the usual string and hair procedure followed. This makes the finished work thicker and less flat than present day work. At present, I am attempting to get an appraisal on the piece.

Bev Klein, Rancher and Artist

***Upon observation of this bridle, Ron Maulding noted the string used to hitch over was string commonly used in the slaughter house and kitchen at Montana State Prison.

Chapter 15

THE HORSEHAIR PRESS

This chapter focuses on the horsehair press – what it is, its use, how to make it, and how to use it.

What a Press is and What it is Used For

As hitching is worked around a dowel, a tube is formed. When hitching is completely slid off the dowel, the result is a long tube. This tube has to be flattened to make a belt. The horsehair press flattens the tube.

A horsehair press is 2 pieces of half inch steel, with nuts and bolts. The hitched tube is put between the 2 pieces of steel, running the length of the press. The nuts and bolts are torqued down to apply pressure on the hitched tube and make it flat.

The word *press* is used in two ways. The two pieces of steel, with nuts and bolts, is called a *press*. It is also used as a verb, as in *press the belt*.

Making a Press

These directions are for making a standard press which should meet most needs. Inlays wider than 2" and belt sizes larger than 42" requires a different press.

Materials needed for a press:

- 2 – metal plates, ½" x 4" x 36"
- 14 – ½" bolts, 2 ½" long; and 14 washers to fit bolts
- 14 – nuts to go with bolts, 1" long
- 2 stainless strips, $^1/_8$ thick, to prevent rust on horsehair products. Read further in this section to understand where the stainless strips go. If stainless steel is not available, or is cost prohibitive, some metal sealers may work.

The two metal plates will be bolted together. Therefore, holes have to be drilled for the bolts. Clamp the two plates together prior to drilling. Carefully mark for placement location. Placement location of drilled holes is: $^9/_{16}$" holes on 5 ¼" centers. See Diagram #15-1 for placement of these drilled holes.

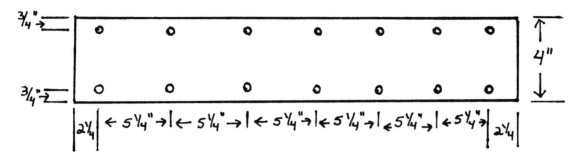

Diagram #15-1
Placement of Drilled Holes

After drilling holes, take one metal plate and put bolts in it. A stainless steel strip will fit between these bolts, and go the length of the metal plate. The stainless steel must lay flat to the plate, or it will interfere with torqueing the press down. Measure for the stainless steel strip and purchase pre-cut.

A metal sealant can be put on the metal plates if you do not use stainless steel strips. Follow manufacturer's directions.

Using a Press

Supplies and Tools for Using a Press

- Paper towels
- Spray bottle of water
- Source of heat
- ½" deep socket wrench
- $^9/_{16}$" wrench
- Potholders

Trim off any loose individual hairs sticking out of the hitched tube. Nothing else needs to be cut off the hitched tube. Lightly spray up and down the outside of the hitched tube with water. Water helps set the press of the belt. ***DO NOT SOAK THE HITCHED TUBE.***

Using your fingers, press the tube flat. Use the cross hitch border as a guide for centering the pattern. If there is not a cross hitch border, center the pattern by eyeing it. Carefully situate the pattern where it should be. If the tube is twisted, straighten it out.

Put the bolts through one metal plate. This will be the bottom of the press.

The hitched blank will run the length of the press. The blank will be sandwiched between the 2 metal plates, now called the press.

Cut 2 layers of paper towel for the bottom of the press. Paper towels should be the width between the bolts, and as long as the hitched blank. Paper towels are used for (1) preventing rust from going on the horsehair; (2) catching any dyed colors that may bleed. Paper towels always go next to the hitched blank.

Center the hitched blank on the paper towels on the press bottom. Make sure nylon string and dropped pulls are *NOT* on the hitched blank. That creates bumps on the pressed blank.

Put 2 layers of paper towels on top of the hitched blank (same measurements as for the bottom paper towels). Put the top of the press on. If you have stainless steel strips, put between paper towels and metal plate. Following is the order in which everything is sandwiched.

METAL PRESS
PAPER TOWELS
HITCHED BLANK
PAPER TOWELS
METAL PRESS

Torque the press down. Put the washers on, and then the nuts. Finger tighten the nuts. Using the wrenches, tighten the nuts. ***Go in a diagonal direction.*** This prevents the hitched blank from slipping inside and being unevenly pressed. See Diagram #15-2.

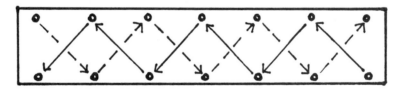

Diagram #15-2
Diagonally Torqueing the Press

Apply heat. Heat helps *set* the press on the hitched blank Heat can be applied by using heat lamps, light bulbs, sunlight, radiators, or any heat vent. Depending on the source of heat, the blank should be left in the press 2 to 4 days. The amount of water sprayed on the hitched blank is also a factor, as the hitched blank dries while in the press.

When applying heat with heat lamps or light bulbs, turn on the heat intermittently and then turn it off. ***Do not leave the press unattended when using heatlamps or light bulbs as a source of heat.***

The more heat, the less time the hitched blank will be in the press.

Periodically tighten the nuts and bolts. As the hitched blank is pressed, nuts and bolts will be loose.

After the first 5 hours or so, the hitched blank can be taken out of the press and checked to see if the pattern is centered where it should be. If it has slipped to one side, spray that area with water and work the blank with your fingers till it is where it should be. Return to the press.

Opinions vary as to what the finished pressed blank should look like and feel like. However, keep in mind that if it looks like plastic and feels like plastic, it is not a collectible art form. You may prefer it that way, but realize it is not collectible. The plastic look and feel is the result of improper pressing, that is torqueing the press too tightly for too long of a time period.

Several days after being out of the press, the blank may relax and not feel as pressed as it was when first taken out of the press. This can be due to humidity and moisture in the air. Repress if necessary.

Some hitchers also use hardwood, such as oak, for their press instead of metal. Problems with wood are:
1. Cannot apply heat source effectively enough for curing time.
2. Wood cannot withstand the compression required to press a hitched horsehair product without eventually splitting.

Tips

- Red dye will bleed most often onto the paper towels. Bleeding of dyes on paper towels is an indication of how well the pulls were rinsed after dyeing. If there is excessive bleeding, rinse the pulls better on the next dye batch.

- Using nuts 1" long are less likely to strip the bolts.

- If the bolt is not threaded enough, use extra washers so the press can be torqued down more.
- Mark the two plates on one end of the press as soon as the holes have been drilled. Always put the press together in the same way.

Chapter 16

INLAYS

This chapter gives general information on hitched horsehair inlays, such as hitching inlays and preparing inlays to place in leather,

Inlays can be used in so many items that specific directions for specific items will not be given.

General Information

Hitched inlays are traditionally inlaid in leather. Historically, inlays started with belts. Other items include, but are not limited to: spur straps, headstalls, checkbook covers, women's hair barrettes, belt buckles, horse breast collars, bracelets, watch bands, bolos, hatbands, rifle slings, guitar straps, wallets, vests, coats, boots, saddles.

Inlays can also be placed in metal. Hitched horsehair inlays are more difficult to work with than stones. Hitched inlays are softer than stones and care has to be taken so the horsehair is not cut into by the metal. One attractive way to use inlays is in sterling silver. We have been making bolos, belt buckles, necklaces, and pins with hitched horsehair inlaid in sterling silver, and believe we are the first to do so. We liken these to the old southwest pawn where each piece was handmade, without any cast silverwork.

Hitching Inlays

Inlays are only 1 thickness of hitching. Imagine a hitched horsehair belt cut down the middle of the back, opened up, and then pressed flat. This is what your inlay will look like. One side has the finished hitched horsehair – what you are used to seeing. The other side shows all the raw ends of the drops, adds, etc. This is what the inside of the hitched tube looks like. Inlays are cut and pressed flat to prevent bulkiness in the finished item.

The finished inlay size determines what size dowel to hitch over. The finished pressed width of the inlay should be approximately 4 times the size of the dowel. Therefore, a ½" dowel will produce a 2" wide inlay; a ⅜" dowel produces a 1 ½" wide inlay; a ⅝" dowel produces a 2 ½" wide inlay; a ¾" dowel produces a 3" wide inlay. Remember, these are approximate widths.

Raw edges are on all sides of the inlay. These edges have to be covered at least ¼" around the inlay. Therefore, the pattern can not be hitched all the way to the edge. Consider the amount of background needed on all sides of the pattern.

Cross hitch borders are usually not on inlays.

When done with the hitching, cut straight down the middle of the back. Flatten out the hitched inlay, and put in the press. This is easier said than done. The inlay will not want to flatten out. Using masking tape, tape both ends of the inlay to the press to hold it down. Depending on the width, use masking tape on the sides also. Put masking tape only where the inlay will be covered later. Masking tape can be hard to get off hitching because of applying heat on the press. Remember the paper towels between the press and hitching.

Spray lightly with water after the masking tape has held down the flattened inlay. Too much water will curl up the hitching. Wipe off any excess water that gets on the press to prevent rusting. Make sure nylon string is not on the hitching or there will be a bump. Add the top layer of paper towel, and put the top of the press on. Work quickly. In spite of the masking tape, the flattened inlay will want to pop up.

Because inlays are only one thickness, they will not have to be in the press as long as other items.

Two Inlays Hitched at the Same Time

Two inlays can be hitched at the same time on the dowel. The start point will be on the side of the hitching – where the cross hitch border normally goes. The chart below shows the counting system with an example of a $^3/_8$" dowel with 2 inlays hitched on one dowel.

```
     34 33 32 31 30 29 28 27 26 25 24 23 22 21
35                                              20
36                                              19
 1                                              18
 2                                              17
      3  4  5  6  7  8  9 10 11 12 13 14 15 16
```

Mark the start point with masking tape. The first inlay will be numbers 1 through 18. Mark number 19 pull with a double knot. The second inlay will be numbers 19 through 36.

There are several advantages to hitching 2 inlays on one dowel:

1. The hitching can be done quicker. If the same pattern is used on both inlays, it is fresh in the hitcher's mind for the second inlay.

2. Pressing is easier. The hitched tube is cut after pressing instead of before. The tube is pressed as it would be for a belt with a cross hitch border. After pressing, cut down both sides where the cross hitch border would be. The result is 2 inlays.

Finishing Inlays

Raw edges are on all sides and the back of the inlay. These edges have to be finished off before it can be inlaid in leather.

Cut off any pulls which show out from under the inlay. Cut off the drop and add pulls to ½" from the hitched inlay backside. Cut off excess nylon string.

Glue a piece of thin leather on the back of the inlay. Use a thin layer of Barge cement, or a similar tacky cement. Too much glue will ooze through to the inlay front.

Cut the desired shape of the inlay. Remember to allow for background hitching so the raw edges will be covered.

The hitched horsehair inlay is ready. Put the inlay in whatever item you are making. Glue the inlay down. Cover the raw edges with leather. Then hand or machine stitch the inlay in place.

Tips

- Use a piece of stiff, see-through plastic to help center the inlay. Cut the plastic the exact shape you want the inlay, including what is under the leather. Center the plastic over the inlay. Cut the hitched inlay the exact shape of the plastic pattern.

Reversible Belt

A reversible belt can be hitched by using the same directions for making two inlays hitched at the same time. Start the belt on the edge with the cross hitch border.

Notes

Chapter 17

HEADSTALLS AND REINS

There are many varieties and styles of headstalls available. The color section of this book shows some collectors' hitched horsehair headstalls and a newer version with leather ends.

Breeds of horses vary enough in size that we are not including particulars in measurements for headstalls. Study the book photos, tack catalogs, and take measurements for your needs and animals. All of the headstall may be hitched, or just a small hitched portion with attached leather ends. That is at your discretion. At this point you have the necessary information to hitch a headstall.

Headstalls may be pressed flat, or hitched over rope. Some headstalls incorporate both, along with braided horsehair. See the next section on reins for hitching over rope and attaching leather to round hitching.

This chapter primarily focuses on making seven foot split reins over one diameter of rope. We refer to other chapters for some of the steps.

There are other lengths and styles, such as roping reins. Study leather or rawhide reins and use this chapter for a base to work with when hitching other rein styles.

General Information

Reins are hitched over $3/16$" diameter nylon rope. The rope stays inside, and the reins will not be pressed. If a black background is being used, the rope may be dyed black.

The finished length of each rein will be 7 feet (excluding tassels). The actual hitching is 6 ½ feet (78 inches). Six inches of the finished length will be leather ends, connecting the reins to the bit. Leather goes on one end. Tassels go on the other end.

Both ends will be covered with knots. Knots cover the joint where leather is sewn to hitching on one end. Knots cover the tassel sewing on the other end.

When hitching, make sure at least 2 ½" of the pull is dropped. You do not want the pull coming out. Also cinch each pull down tight. Reins are not pressed, and pulls need to lay flat.

Hitching Information

There are 20 pulls per row. Background pulls can be all closed hitch as it cinches down tighter. Patterns *in the round* will be done with open and closed hitches.

Spiral hitching with different colors by using all closed hitches creates very attractive reins.

Hitching 6 ½ feet per rein is for fully hitched reins. At your discretion, less hitching can be done with more leather showing.

Preparing Hitching for Sewing to Leather and Tassels

Cut the nylon rope as flush to the hitching as possible. **CAREFULLY** sear the rope with a match. **DO NOT** burn the hitching. Duco cement the end of the rope. Secure the nylon string with needle and thread. Cut it off. Duco cement the end of the string.

Leather Ends

These directions are for 1 rein. Repeat these directions for the other rein. See Chapter 12, *Leather Belt Ends,* if some of these terms seem unfamiliar.

The leather on the bit end measures 6" from the knot to the foldover. An additional 3 ½" extends beyond the foldover for securing the Chicago screws. When measuring the finished length remember some leather will be under the knot.

The rein end will be sandwiched between two pieces of 4-5 ounce leather. Cut two pieces of leather 11 ¼" long and $^9/_{16}$" wide. Only 1 ¼" of the leather will go over the hitched rein. The remaining leather will be glued together. See Diagram #17-1.

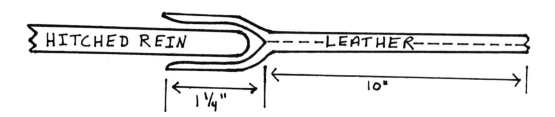

Diagram #17-1
Rein Attached to Leather End

The 1 ¼" that will not be glued together needs to be skived on the edges and end. This prevents a large lump under the knot when the leather is sewn to the reins.

The foldover end also needs to be skived on the end only (similar to foldover on a belt). Skive the inside part of the leather where it is glued together.

Using a #3 edger, round off the long edges.

Dye the face, back, and sides of the leather. Edge Kote the sides after dye dries.

Barge cement the 2 pieces of leather together *UP TO 1 ¼" FROM THE END THAT ATTACHES TO THE REIN.* See Diagram #17-2 (side view).

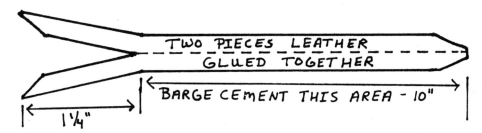

Diagram #17-2
Barge Cementing Leather Together (Side View)

The stitch line is $1/8$" in from the edge. Stitch only the glued part of the leather. See Diagram #17-3. Poke 2 holes in the leather where it will be sewn to the reins. The holes go in the 1 ¼" part that was not glued together. See Diagram #17-3.

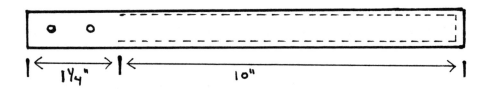

Diagram #17-3
Stitch Line for Rein Leather Ends (Top View)

Finish the edges with beeswax.

Sandwich the rein between the 2 parts of leather that were not glued together. Using strong thread, sew leather tightly to the rein. See Diagram #17-4 for this process. The diagram is loosely drawn so you can better see where the thread goes.

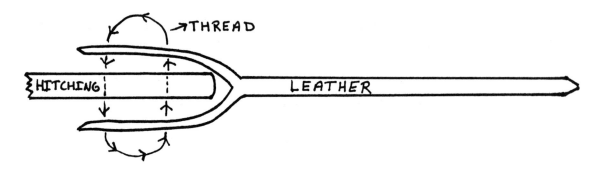

Diagram #17-4
Sewing Leather to Reins (Side View)

Wet the leather and wrap tightly with wide string. The leather will mold to the reins. Set aside to dry, 3 to 4 days.

Knot over this joint.

Chicago Screws and Foldover on the Opposite Leather End

Measure for a 7' rein. Fold over the leather at that point. Punch 2 holes for 2 Chicago screws. Two Chicago screws hold better than one. Put the first screw about $1\,^5/_8$" from the foldover. Put the other screw towards the skived leather end so the leather will not be able to fold back on itself as the reins are used.

Tassels

Four to seven inch tassels are on the other end, where the rider holds the reins.

Tassels should be full to look nice. For full tassels, use both these methods to finish:

1. When hitching the last couple of inches, have the pulls long so when they are dropped out they can be part of the tassel. Add new pulls where necessary to accomplish this.

2. Add additional pulls after the hitching is completed. Make 20 pulls with 20 hairs per pull. At the midpoint of each pull, sew each pull to the last hitched row of the rein. See Diagram #17-5.

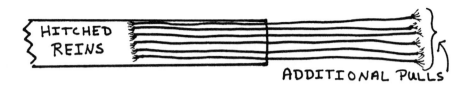

Diagram #17-5
Sewing Additional Pulls for Tassels

When all 20 pulls have been sewn at midpoint onto the last row, double over the pulls. Secure the pulls with thread. *Duco cement the area. DO NOT just lay the pulls in straight, or the hairs will fall out.* The pulls need to be doubled over. See Diagram #17-6 (loosely drawn).

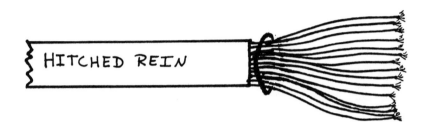

Diagram #17-6
Doubling over Additional Pulls for Tassels

Adding 20 pulls in this way adds an additional 800 hairs for the tassel. Any color may be used.

Cut off the short hairs in the tassel so there will be only one length of hair.

Cover this area with a knot. A nice bell shape will be formed because of how the additional tassels were added.

Cut tassels 4" to 7". Using fingers, separate the individual hairs and fluff them out.

Tips

♦ Spray water on the hitched reins and roll with a rolling pin motion. This sets the pulls in place.

Notes

Chapter 18

HISTORY

The history of hitched horsehair is, at best, sketchy.

The use of horsehair dates back to the Moors who conquered Spain in the 8th century. Spaniards brought this art to the New World where it was refined. Cowboys, Indians, Mexicans, sheepherders, and prison inmates have primarily worked horsehair.

The history of hitching is intertwined with the history of territorial and modern day prisons in the western United States. Hitched horsehair is a time consuming art, and who better than inmates have time on their hands. Bridles and belts were very popular items, and even the fashionable gentleman's cane was hitched. Finished products were sold, traded, or given away. Most hitchers on the *outside*, meaning outside of prison walls, have learned from inmates or have a prison connection in some way.

Hitched horsehair was the first hobby at Montana, dating back to the old territorial prison days. Other prisons known for horsehair were located at Yuma, Arizona; Rawlins, Wyoming; and Walla Walla, Washington.

Some experts on horsehair can date and tell where an object was made by the colors. At various times in prisons, commercial dyes were not available. Natural hair colors were used then. Or some colored dyes were used in some areas more than others.

As inmates would come and go from prison, hitching would cycle in and out, to the extent of being almost a lost art. Once an inmate discharged (finished all his time), or was paroled, he usually discontinued hitching. The ex-inmate no longer had the time for both hitching and providing a living for himself. Hitching also requires discipline, and once outside prison walls he had freedom to do other things that were unavailable while in prison. Hitching was usually dropped.

Everything has a value on it in prison, including knowledge. Inmates can not have money inside, nor can they directly pay another inmate. There is an elaborate barter or exchange system. Some inmates have paid up to $1,000 to learn how to hitch. This price can include having the *student* make 3,000 pulls for the *teacher* before hitching lessons even begin.

Hobby programs in prisons have changed since the 1800's territorial prisons. But the purpose has remained the same. Allowing hobby keeps the inmates busy, which creates less pressure and less trouble inside. Hobby also builds self-esteem, which reduces tension. A study done in California in 1987 showed that inmates who did hobby more than 6 months were 51% less likely to return to prison.

Other research concluded that inmates participating in art programs showed a 70 to 80% reduction in violent and other disruptive behavior while in prison.

Hitched horsehair is presently enjoying a resurgence both among collectors and hitchers. This is a positive direction for hitching, which was almost a lost art. People with old pieces are asking questions and trying to find answers. We know of one collectible bridle owned by an Idaho rancher where sinew was used as a core material.

As the public sees more of both old and new pieces, awareness of this art increases. Hitchers and non-hitchers alike are in awe that such a common material can make such exquisite items.

Hitched horsehair need not be worn only by "Westerners" or with western clothes. Given the price and the elegance of hitching, it is being worn and displayed in all facets of life.

With increased public awareness about hitching, more old pieces are surfacing. This helps to fill in the missing pieces of the history of this art.

We welcome your stories, photos, and informative comments. Let us know if we can use any of these in future publications.

Chapter 19

ODDS AND ENDS

This chapter is for all those odds and ends that just don't fit in anywhere else.

Tips for Buying Hitched Horsehair

The following information are tips and guidelines for buying new high-quality, collectible hitched horsehair.

- Look for uniformity in hitching. Patterns should be centered from edge to edge, and lengthwise. Hitching tension is the tightness of the hitched rows, usually 8 ½" to 10 ½" rows per inch of hitching. Being consistent in hitching tension is more important than the amount of rows hitched per inch.

- Dyed colors should not bleed into other colors or background.

- A stray hair poking out here or there is acceptable. Just cut it off. Many hairs poking out is poor quality work.

- If the item looks like plastic and feels like plastic, it is not considered collectible by serious collectors. It has been improperly pressed.

- Pulls of hair should be laying down.

- Attached leather ends should be of standard lengths; i.e. 3" showing on the buckle end, and 8-9" on the tongue end. Excessive leather with a short, hitched blank is not collectible.

- Choose colors and designs that are personally pleasing to you.

Necessity is the Mother of Inventions

Sometimes supplies and tools are not accessible. When inside a prison, on a trail ride, or building a house, and everything isn't readily available, it's time to innovate.

Substitute:

> A pencil for a dowel
> Bed springs and mattress for a press
> Radiator or heat duct for heat lamps
> Sunshine for heat lamps
> Nail clippers for scissors
> Paper or the top half off a peroxide bottle for a funnel

Restoration Work

When others discover you hitch, you'll probably be asked to do restoration work. There is some work that is impossible to restore unless a whole new piece is hitched. The hitched item is usually more valuable if left as it is. Learn to say *NO*.

Chapter 20

COMPLETE PATTERNS AND DIRECTIONS

This chapter gives complete patterns and directions for those patterns. Patterns are graphed out. Directions are for face pulls only.

In order to make this book affordable, letters will designate colors used in these pattern directions. Color codes are on each pattern. Any colors can be used in place of the colors in these pattern directions.

In open hitch rows, letters will be on the graph paper line. In closed hitch rows, letters will be in the middle of the square. This is where the colored lines go.

These abbreviations are used:
- op or Op = open hitch
- cl or Cl = closed hitch
- st or St = stand or standing
- bgrd = background

Using the knowledge gained from other chapters, count from start point to the first cross hitch border. Follow the directions in this chapter for face pulls. Then count from the second cross hitch border to the end of the row.

To make it easier, graph the patterns out on your own graph paper. Color in the pattern colors. As a learning exercise, figure out what hitching steps to take in each row. Write those steps down. Then compare with what is in the book.

Some patterns have the same outside shape, but the inside colors are arranged differently. This shows the creativity and uniqueness you can bring to each hitched item.

The narrower patterns can be used on wider belt widths. Adjust the background pulls accordingly.

Put notes on your graph paper that help when reading the graph paper. Notes such as *st, drop,* or *add*, next to the pattern lines help.

Pattern #101-A

Row	
1	op
2	cl
3	op
4	cl
5	op
6	cl
7	op
8	cl
9	op
10	cl
11	op
12	cl
13	op
14	cl
15	op
16	cl
17	op
18	cl
19	op
20	cl
21	op
22	cl
23	op
24	cl
25	op
26	cl
27	op
28	cl
29	op

R = Red
B = Blue
G = Gold

Directions for Pattern #101-A

Note: Add bgrd in these directions means to add one background pull. *Drop bgrd* in directions means to drop one background pull. *St bgrd* means to stand one background pull.

Row 1. Op 11 bgrd. Add red. Op 11 bgrd.

Row 2. Cl 10 bgrd to where bgrd and red are in same hole. Drop bgrd. Cl red. Add red. St bgrd. Cl 10 bgrd.

Row 3. Op 10 bgrd. Cl red. Add blue. Op red. Drop st bgrd. Op 10 bgrd.

Row 4. Cl 9 bgrd to where bgrd and red are in same hole. Drop bgrd. Cl red, blue. Add blue. Op red. St bgrd. Cl 9 bgrd.

Row 5. Op 9 bgrd. Cl red, blue. Add gold. Op blue, red. Drop st bgrd. Op 9 bgrd.

Row 6. Cl 8 bgrd to where bgrd and red are in same hole. Drop bgrd. Cl red, blue, gold. Add gold. Op blue, red. St bgrd. Cl 8 bgrd.

Row 7. Op 8 bgrd. Cl red, blue, gold. Add blue. Op gold, blue, red. Drop st bgrd. Op 8 bgrd.

Row 8. Cl 7 bgrd to where bgrd and red are in same hole. Drop bgrd. Cl red, blue, gold, blue. Add blue. Op gold, blue, red. St bgrd. Cl 7 bgrd.

Row 9. Op 7 bgrd. Cl red, blue, gold, blue. Add red. Op blue, gold, blue, red. Drop st bgrd. Op 7 bgrd.

Row 10. Cl 6 bgrd to where bgrd and red are in same hole. Drop bgrd. Cl red, blue, gold, blue, red. Add red. Op blue, gold, blue, red. St bgrd. Cl 6 bgrd.

Row 11. Op 6 bgrd. Cl red, blue, gold, blue, red. Add blue. Op red, blue, gold, blue, red. Drop st bgrd. Op 6 bgrd.

Row 12. Cl 5 bgrd to where bgrd and red are in same hole. Drop bgrd. Cl red, blue, gold, blue, red, blue. Add blue. Op red, blue, gold, blue, red. St bgrd. Cl 5 bgrd.

Row 13. Op 5 bgrd. Cl red, blue, gold, blue, red, blue. Add gold. Op blue, red, blue, gold, blue, red. Drop st bgrd. Op 5 bgrd.

Row 14. Cl 4 bgrd to where bgrd and red are in same hole. Drop bgrd. Cl red, blue, gold, blue, red, blue, gold. Add gold. Op blue, red, blue, gold, blue, red. St bgrd. Cl 4 bgrd.

Row 15. Op 4 bgrd. Cl red, blue, gold, blue, red, blue, gold. Add red. Op gold, blue, red, blue, gold, blue, red. Drop st bgrd. Op 4 bgrd.

Row 16. Cl 3 bgrd to where bgrd and red are in same hole. Drop bgrd. Cl red, blue, gold, blue, red, blue, gold, red. Add red. Op gold, blue, red, blue, gold, blue, red. St bgrd. Cl 3 bgrd.

Row 17. Op 3 bgrd. Cl red, blue, gold, blue, red, blue, gold, red. Add blue. Op red, gold, blue, red, blue, gold, blue, red. Drop st bgrd. Op 3 bgrd.

Row 18. Cl 2 bgrd to where bgrd and red are in same hole. Drop bgrd. Cl red, blue, gold, blue, red, blue, gold, red, blue. Add blue. Op red, gold, blue, red, blue, gold, blue, red. St bgrd. Cl 2 bgrd.

Row 19. Op 2 bgrd. Add bgrd. Op red, blue, gold, blue, red, blue, gold. St red. Cl blue. Add gold. Op blue. St red. Cl gold, blue, red, blue, gold, blue, red. Drop st bgrd. Add bgrd. Op 2 bgrd.

Row 20. Cl 1 bgrd to where 2 bgrd in same hole. Cl 1 bgrd; op 1 bgrd. Op red, blue, gold, blue, red, blue. St gold. Drop st red. Cl blue, gold. Add gold. Op blue. Drop st red. St gold. Cl blue, red, blue, gold, blue, red. Cl 3 bgrd.

Row 21. Op 3 bgrd. Add bgrd. Op red, blue, gold, blue, red, blue. Drop st gold. St blue. Cl gold. Add bgrd. Op gold, blue. Drop st gold. St blue. Cl red, blue, gold, blue, red. Add bgrd. Op 3 bgrd.

Row 22. Cl 2 bgrd to where 2 bgrd in same hole. Cl 1 bgrd; op 1 bgrd. Op red, blue, gold, blue, red. St blue. Drop st blue. Cl gold. Cl 1 bgrd. Add bgrd. Op gold. St blue. Drop st blue, Cl red, blue, gold, blue, red. Cl 4 bgrd.

Row 23. Op 4 bgrd. Add bgrd. Op red, blue, gold, blue. St red. Drop st blue. Cl gold. Add bgrd. Op 2 bgrd. Op gold. Drop st blue. St red. Cl blue, gold, blue, red. Add bgrd. Op 4 bgrd.

Row 24. Cl 3 bgrd to where 2 bgrd in same hole. Cl 1 bgrd; op 1 bgrd. Op red, blue, gold. St blue. Drop st red. Cl gold. Cl 3 bgrd. Add bgrd. Op gold. Drop st red. St blue. Cl gold, blue, red. Cl 5 bgrd.

Row 25. Op 5 bgrd. Add bgrd. Op red, blue. St gold. Drop st blue. Cl gold. Add bgrd. Op 4 bgrd. Op gold. Drop st blue. St gold. Cl blue, red. Add bgrd. Op 5 bgrd.

Row 26. Cl 4 bgrd to where 2 bgrd in same hole. Cl 1 bgrd; op 1 bgrd. Op red. St blue. Drop st gold. Cl gold. Cl 5 bgrd. Add bgrd. Op gold. Drop st gold. St blue. Cl red. Cl 6 bgrd.

Row 27. Op 6 bgrd. Add bgrd. Op red. Drop st blue. St gold. Add bgrd. Op 6 bgrd. St gold. Drop st blue. Cl red. Add bgrd. Op 6 bgrd.

Row 28. Cl 5 bgrd to where 2 bgrd in same hole. Cl 1 bgrd; op 1 bgrd. St red. Drop st gold. Cl 7 bgrd. Add bgrd. Drop st gold. St red. Cl 7 bgrd.

Row 29. Op 7 bgrd. Drop st red. Op 8 bgrd. Drop st red. Op 7 bgrd.

Pattern #101-B

Row	Pattern
1 op	* * * * 7 * * * / * * * 8 * * * / * * * 7 * * * *
2 cl	R * * * * 7 * * * R
3 op	R G * * * 6 * * G R * * * 6 * *
4 cl	R B G * * 5 * * G B R
5 op	R B G G * * 4 * G G B R * * * 5 * *
6 cl	R B G B G * 3 * G B G B R
7 op	R B G B R G * 2 * G R B G B R * * * 4 *
8 cl	R B G B R B G * G B R B G B R
9 op	R B G B R B B G G B B R B G B R * * 3 *
10 cl	R B G B R B G B G B G B R B G B R
11 op	R B G B R B G R B B R G B R B G B R * 2 *
12 cl	R B G B R B G R B R G B R B G B R
13 op	R B G B R B G R R G B R B G B R * * 3 *
14 cl	R B G B R B G R G B R B G B R
15 op	R B G B R B G G B R B G B R * * * 4 *
16 cl	R B G B R B G B R B G B R
17 op	R B G B R B B R B G B R * * * 5 *
18 cl	R B G B R B R B G B R
19 op	R B G B R R B G B R * * * 6 * *
20 cl	R B G B R B G B R
21 op	R B G B B G B R * * * * 7 * *
22 cl	R B G B G B R
23 op	R B G G B R * * * * 8 * * *
24 cl	R B G B R
25 op	R B B R * * * * 9 * * *
26 cl	R B R
27 op	R R * * * * * * * 10 * *
28 cl	R
29 op	* * * * * * 11 * * * * / * * * * * * 11 * * * * *

R = Red
B = Blue
G = Gold

Directions for Pattern #101-B

Note: Add bgrd in these directions means to add one background pull. *Drop bgrd* in directions means to drop one background pull. *St bgrd* means to stand one background pull.

Row 1. Op 7 bgrd. Add red. Op 8 bgrd. Add red. Op 7 bgrd.

Row 2. Cl 6 bgrd to where bgrd and red are in same hole. Drop bgrd. Cl red. Add gold. St bgrd. Cl 6 bgrd. Add gold. Bgrd and red in same hole. Drop bgrd. Op red. St bgrd. Cl 6 bgrd.

Row 3. Op 6 bgrd. Cl red. Add blue. Op gold. Drop st bgrd. Op 6 bgrd. Cl gold. Add blue. Op red. Drop st bgrd. Op 6 bgrd.

Row 4. Cl 5 bgrd to where bgrd and red are in same hole. Drop bgrd. Cl red, blue. Add gold. Op gold. St bgrd. Cl 4 bgrd. Bgrd and gold in same hole. Drop bgrd. Cl gold. Add gold. Op blue, red. St bgrd. Cl 5 bgrd.

Row 5. Op 5 bgrd. Cl red, blue, gold. Add blue. Op gold. Drop st bgrd. Op 4 bgrd. Cl gold. Add blue. Op gold, blue, red. Drop st bgrd. Op 5 bgrd.

Row 6. Cl 4 bgrd to where bgrd and red are in same hole. Drop bgrd. Cl red, blue, gold, blue. Add red. Op gold. St bgrd. Cl 2 bgrd. Bgrd and gold in same hole. Drop bgrd. Cl gold. Add red. Op blue, gold, blue, red. St bgrd. Cl 4 bgrd.

Row 7. Op 4 bgrd. Cl red, blue, gold, blue, red. Add blue. Op gold. Drop st bgrd. Op 2 bgrd. Cl gold. Add blue. Op red, blue, gold, blue, red. Drop st bgrd. Op 4 bgrd.

Row 8. Cl 3 bgrd to where bgrd and red are in same hole. Drop bgrd. Cl red, blue, gold, blue, red, blue. Add blue. Op gold. St bgrd. Bgrd and gold in same hole. Drop bgrd. Cl gold, blue. Add blue. Op red, blue, gold, blue, red. St bgrd. Cl 3 bgrd.

Row 9. Op 3 bgrd. Cl red, blue, gold, blue, red, blue. Add gold. Op blue, gold. Drop st bgrd. St gold. Cl blue. Add gold. Op blue, red, blue, gold, blue, red. Drop st bgrd. Op 3 bgrd.

Row 10. Cl 2 bgrd to where bgrd and red are in same hole. Drop bgrd. Cl red, blue, gold, blue, red, blue, gold. Add red. Op blue. St gold. Drop st gold. Cl blue. Add red. Op gold, blue, red, blue, gold, blue, red. St bgrd. Cl 2 bgrd.

Row 11. Op 2 bgrd. Add bgrd. Op red, blue, gold, blue, red, blue, gold, red, blue. Drop st gold. St blue. Cl red, gold, blue, red, blue, gold, blue, red. Drop st bgrd. Add bgrd. Op 2 bgrd.

Row 12. Cl 1 bgrd to where 2 bgrd in same hole. Cl 1 bgrd; op 1 bgrd. Op red, blue, gold, blue, red, blue, gold, red. St blue. Drop st blue. Cl red, gold, blue, red, blue, gold, blue, red. Cl 3 bgrd.

Row 13. Op 3 bgrd. Add bgrd. Op red, blue, gold, blue, red, blue, gold, red. Drop st blue. St red. Cl gold, blue, red, blue, gold, blue, red. Add bgrd. Op 3 bgrd.

Row 14. Cl 2 bgrd to where 2 bgrd in same hole Cl 1 bgrd; op 1 bgrd. Op red, blue, gold, blue, red, blue, gold. St red. Drop st red. Cl gold, blue, red, blue, gold, blue, red. Cl 4 bgrd.

Row 15. Op 4 bgrd. Add bgrd. Op red, blue, gold, blue, red, blue, gold. Drop st red. St gold. Cl blue, red, blue, gold, blue, red. Add bgrd. Op 4 bgrd.

Row 16. Cl 3 bgrd to where 2 bgrd in same hole. Cl 1 bgrd; op 1 bgrd. Op red, blue, gold, blue, red, blue. St gold. Drop st gold. Cl blue, red, blue, gold, blue, red. Cl 5 bgrd.

Row 17. Op 5 bgrd. Add bgrd. Op red, blue, gold, blue, red, blue. Drop st gold. St blue. Cl red, blue, gold, blue, red. Add bgrd. Op 5 bgrd.

Row 18. Cl 4 bgrd to where 2 bgrd in same hole. Cl 1 bgrd; op 1 bgrd. Op red, blue, gold, blue, red. St blue. Drop st blue. Cl red, blue, gold, blue, red. Cl 6 bgrd.

Row 19. Op 6 bgrd. Add bgrd. Op red, blue, gold, blue, red. Drop st blue. St red, Cl blue, gold, blue, red. Add bgrd. Op 6 bgrd.

Row 20. Cl 5 bgrd to where 2 bgrd in same hole. Cl 1 bgrd; op 1 bgrd. Op red, blue, gold, blue. St red. Drop st red. Cl blue, gold, blue, red. Cl 7 bgrd.

Row 21. Op 7 bgrd. Add bgrd. Op red, blue, gold, blue. Drop st red. St blue. Cl gold, blue, red. Add bgrd. Op 7 bgrd.

Row 22. Cl 6 bgrd to where 2 bgrd in same hole. Cl 1 bgrd; op 1 bgrd. Op red, blue, gold. St blue. Drop st blue. Cl gold, blue, red. Cl 8 bgrd.

Row 23. Op 8 bgrd. Add bgrd. Op red, blue, gold. Drop st blue. St gold. Cl blue, red. Add bgrd. Op 8 bgrd.

Row 24. Cl 7 bgrd to where 2 bgrd in same hole. Cl 1 bgrd; op 1 bgrd. Op red, blue. St gold. Drop st gold. Cl blue, red. Cl 9 bgrd.

Row 25. Op 9 bgrd. Add bgrd. Op red, blue. Drop st gold. St blue. Cl red. Add bgrd. Op 9 bgrd.

Row 26. Cl 8 bgrd to where 2 bgrd in same hole. Cl 1 bgrd; op 1 bgrd. Op red. St blue. Drop st blue. Cl red. Cl 10 bgrd.

Row 27. Op 10 bgrd. Add bgrd. Op red. Drop st blue. St red. Add bgrd. Op 10 bgrd.

Row 28. Cl 9 bgrd to where 2 bgrd in same hole. Cl 1 bgrd; op 1 bgrd. St red. Drop st red. Cl 11 bgrd.

Row 29. Op 11 bgrd. Drop st red. Op 11 bgrd.

Pattern #102-A

A triangular charted pattern on grid paper, 29 rows numbered on the right (alternating "op" and "cl"):

Row	Pattern	Side
1	* * * * * * *11* * * * */* * * * * * * *11* * * *	op
2	B	cl
3	R R * * * * * * *10* * *	op
4	R G R	cl
5	R G G R * * * * * *9* * *	op
6	R G B G R	cl
7	R G B B G R * * * *8* * *	op
8	R G B R B G R	cl
9	R G B R R B G R * * *7* * *	op
10	R G B R B R B G R	cl
11	R G B R B B R B G R * * * *6* *	op
12	R B G B R B R B G B R	cl
13	R B B G B R R B G B B R * * *5* *	op
14	R B R B G B R B G B R B R	cl
15	R B R R B G B B G B R R B R * *4* *	op
16	R B R B R B G B G B R B R B R	cl
17	R G R B B R B G G B R B B R B R *3* *	op
18	R B R B G B R G B R B G B R B R	cl
2 19	R B R B G G B R G B R B G G B R B R *2*	op
20	R B R B G B R B R B R B G B R B R	cl
21	R B R B B R B R R B R B B R B R * *3*	op
22	R B R B R B R * R B R B R B R	cl
23	R B R R B R *2* R B R R B R * * *4*	op
24	R B R B R * *3* R B R B R	cl
25	R G B R * *4* * R G B R * * *5* *	op
26	R B R * * *5* * R B R	cl
27	R R * * *6* * * R R * * *6* * *	op
28	R * * * *7* * * R	cl
29	* * *7* * * */* * * * *8* * * */* * * *7* * *	op

R = Red
B = Blue
G = Gold

Directions for Pattern #102-A

Patterns #102-A and #102-B have the same outside shape as #101-A and #101-B. However, the inside of the patterns are totally different. This is an example of the uniqueness each shape can have. Other colors will also create a totally different look.

Note: Add bgrd in these directions means to add one background pull. *Drop background* in directions means to drop one background pull. *St bgrd* means to stand one background pull.

Row 1. Op 11 bgrd. Add red. Op 11 bgrd.

Row 2. Cl 10 bgrd to where bgrd and red are in same hole. Drop bgrd. Cl red. Add red. St bgrd. Cl 10 bgrd.

Row 3. Op 10 bgrd. Cl red. Add gold. Op red. Drop st bgrd. Op 10 bgrd.

Row 4. Cl 9 bgrd to where bgrd and red are in same hole. Drop bgrd. Cl red, gold. Add gold. Op red. St bgrd. Cl 9 bgrd.

Row 5. Op 9 bgrd. Cl red, gold. Add blue. Op gold, red. Drop st bgrd. Op 9 bgrd.

Row 6. Cl 8 bgrd to where bgrd and red are in same hole. Drop bgrd. Cl red, gold, blue. Add blue. Op gold, red. St bgrd. Cl 8 bgrd.

Row 7. Op 8 bgrd. Cl red, gold, blue. Add red. Op blue, gold, red. Drop st bgrd. Op 8 bgrd.

Row 8. Cl 7 bgrd to where bgrd and red are in same hole. Drop bgrd. Cl red, gold, blue, red. Add red. Op blue, gold, red. St bgrd. Cl 7 bgrd.

Row 9. Op 7 bgrd. Cl red, gold, blue, red. Add blue. Op red, blue, gold, red. Drop st bgrd. Op 7 bgrd.

Row 10. Cl 6 bgrd to where bgrd and red are in same hole. Drop bgrd. Cl red, gold, blue, red, blue. Add blue. Op red, blue, gold, red. St bgrd. Cl 6 bgrd.

Row 11. Op 6 bgrd. Cl red. Add blue. Op gold, blue, red. St blue. Cl blue, red, blue, gold. Add blue. Op red. Drop st bgrd. Op 6 bgrd.

Row 12. Cl 5 bgrd to where bgrd and red are in same hole. Drop bgrd. Cl red, blue. Add blue. Op gold, blue, red. Drop st blue. St blue. Cl red, blue, gold, blue. Add blue. Op red. St bgrd. Cl 5 bgrd.

Row 13. Op 5 bgrd. Cl red, blue. Add red. Op blue, gold, blue, red. Drop st blue. St red. Cl blue, gold, blue. Add red. Op blue, red. Drop st bgrd. Op 5 bgrd.

Row 14. Cl 4 bgrd to where bgrd and red are in same hole. Drop bgrd. Cl red, blue, red. Add red. Op blue, gold, blue. St red. Drop st red. Cl blue, gold, blue, red. Add red. Op blue, red. St bgrd. Cl 4 bgrd.

Row 15. Op 4 bgrd. Cl red, blue, red. Add blue. Op red, blue, gold, blue. Drop st red. St blue. Cl gold, blue, red. Add blue. Op red, blue, red. Drop st bgrd. Op 4 bgrd.

Row 16. Cl 3 bgrd to where bgrd and red are in same hole. Drop bgrd. Cl red, blue, red, blue. Add blue. Op red, blue, gold. St blue. Drop st blue. Cl gold, blue, red, blue. Add blue. Op red, blue, red. St bgrd. Cl 3 bgrd.

Row 17. Op 3 bgrd. Cl red, blue, red, blue. Add gold. Op blue, red, blue, gold. Drop st blue. St gold. Cl blue, red, blue. Add gold. Op blue, red, blue, red. Drop st bgrd. Op 3 bgrd.

Row 18. Cl 2 bgrd to where bgrd and red are in same hole. Drop bgrd. Cl red, blue, red, blue, gold. Add god. Op blue, red, blue. St gold. Drop st gold. Cl blue, red, blue, gold. Add gold. Op blue, red, blue, red. St bgrd. Cl 2 bgrd.

Row 19. Op 2 bgrd. Add bgrd. Op red, blue, red, blue. St gold. Cl gold, blue, red, blue. Drop st gold. Add red. Op blue, red, blue. St gold. Cl gold, blue, red, blue, red. Drop st bgrd. Add bgrd. Op 2 bgrd.

Row 20. Cl 1 bgrd to where 2 bgrd in same hole. Cl 1 bgrd; op 1 bgrd. Op red, blue, red, blue. Drop st gold. St gold. Cl blue, red, blue, red. Add red. Op blue, red, blue. Drop st gold. St gold. Cl blue, red, blue, red. Cl 3 bgrd.

Row 21. Op 3 bgrd. Add bgrd. Op red, blue, red blue. Drop st gold. St blue. Cl red, blue, red. Add bgrd. Op red, blue, red, blue. Drop st gold. St blue. Cl red, blue, red. Add bgrd. Op 3 bgrd.

Row 22. Cl 2 bgrd to where 2 bgrd in same hole. Cl 1 bgrd; op 1 bgrd. Op red, blue, red. St blue. Drop st blue. Cl red, blue, red. Cl 1 bgrd. Add bgrd. Op red, blue, red. St blue. Drop st blue. Cl red, blue, red. Cl 4 bgrd.

Row 23. Op 4 bgrd. Add bgrd. Op red, blue, red. Drop st blue. St red. Cl blue, red. Add bgrd. Op 2 bgrd. Op red, blue, red. Drop st blue. St red. Cl blue, red. Add bgrd. Op 4 bgrd.

Row 24. Cl 3 bgrd to where 2 bgrd in same hole. Cl 1 bgrd; op 1 bgrd. Op red, blue. St red. Drop st red. Cl blue, red. Cl 3 bgrd. Add bgrd. Op red, blue. St red. Drop st red. Cl blue, red. Cl 5 bgrd.

Row 25. Op 5 bgrd. Add bgrd. Op red, blue. Drop st red. St blue. Cl red. Add bgrd. Op 4 bgrd. Op red, blue. Drop st red. St blue. Cl red. Add bgrd. Op 5 bgrd.

Row 26. Cl 4 bgrd to where 2 bgrd in same hole. Cl 1 bgrd; op 1 bgrd. Op red. St blue. Drop st blue. Cl red. Cl 5 bgrd. Add bgrd. Op red. St blue. Drop st blue. Cl red. Cl 6 bgrd.

Row 27. Op 6 bgrd. Add bgrd. Op red. Drop st blue. St red. Add bgrd. Op 6 bgrd. Op red. Drop st blue. St red. Add bgrd. Op 6 bgrd.

Row 28. Cl 5 bgrd to where 2 bgrd in same hole. Cl 1 bgrd; op 1 bgrd. St red. Drop st red. Cl 7 bgrd. Add bgrd. St red. Drop st red. Cl 7 bgrd.

Row 29. Op 7 bgrd. Drop st red. Op 8 bgrd. Drop st red. Op 7 bgrd.

Pattern #102-B

Row	Pattern	Side
1	x x x x 7 x x x / x x x x 8 x x x / x x x x 7 x x x	op
2	R x x x x 7 x x x R	cl
3	R R x x x x 6 x x R R x x x x 6 x x	op
4	R B R x x 5 x x R B R	cl
5	R B B R x x x 4 x R B B R x x x x 5 x	op
6	R B R B R x 3 x R B R B R	cl
7	R B R R B R x 2 x R B R R B R x x x 4 x	op
8	R B R B R B R x R B R B R B R	cl
9	R B R B B R B R R B R B B R B R x x 3 x	op
10	R B R B G B R B R B G B R B R	cl
11	R B R B G G B R B B R B G G B R B R x 2 x	op
12	R B R B G B R B G B R B G B R B R	cl
13	R B R B B R B G G B R B R B R x x 3 x	op
14	R B R B R B G B G B R B R B R	cl
15	R B R R B G B B G B R R B R x x x 4 x	op
16	R B R B G B R B G B R B R	cl
17	R B B G B R R B G B B R x x x x 5 x	op
18	R B G B R B R B G B R	cl
19	R G B R G B R B G R x x x 6 x x	op
20	R G B R B R B G R	cl
21	R G B R R B G R x x x x 7 x x	op
22	R G B R B G R	cl
23	R G B B G R x x x x 8 x x	op
24	R G B G R	cl
25	R G G R x x x x 9 x x	op
26	R G R	cl
27	R R x x x x 10 x x x	op
28	R	cl
29	x x x x 11 x x x / x x x x x 11 x x x	op

R = Red
B = Blue
G = Gold

Directions for Pattern #102-B

Note: Add bgrd in these directions means to add one background pull. *Drop bgrd* in directions means to drop one background pull. *St bgrd* means to stand one background pull.

Row 1. Op 7 bgrd. Add red. Op 8 bgrd. Add red. Op 7 bgrd.

Row 2. Cl 6 bgrd to where bgrd and red in same hole. Drop bgrd. Cl red. Add red. St bgrd. Cl 6 bgrd. Bgrd and red in same hole. Drop bgrd. Cl red. Add red. St bgrd. Cl 6 bgrd.

Row 3. Op 6 bgrd. Cl red. Add blue. Op red. Drop st bgrd. Op 6 bgrd. Cl red. Add blue. Op red. Drop st bgrd. Op 6 bgrd.

Row 4. Cl 5 bgrd to where bgrd and red in same hole. Drop bgrd. Cl red, blue. Add blue. Op red. St bgrd. Cl 4 bgrd. Bgrd and red in same hole. Drop bgrd. Cl red, blue. Add blue. Op red. St bgrd. Cl 5 bgrd.

Row 5. Op 5 bgrd. Cl red, blue. Add red. Op blue, red. Drop st bgrd. Op 4 bgrd. Cl red, blue. Add red. Op blue, red. Drop st bgrd. Op 5 bgrd.

Row 6. Cl 4 bgrd to where bgrd and red in same hole. Drop bgrd. Cl red, blue, red. Add red. Op blue, red. St bgrd. Cl 2 bgrd. Bgrd and red in same hole. Drop bgrd. Cl red, blue, red. Add red. Op blue, red. St bgrd. Cl 4 bgrd.

Row 7. Op 4 bgrd. Cl red, blue, red. Add blue. Op red, blue, red. Drop st bgrd. Op 2 bgrd. Cl red, blue, red. Add blue. Op red, blue, red. Drop st bgrd. Op 4 bgrd.

Row 8. Cl 3 bgrd to where bgrd and red in same hole. Drop bgrd. Cl red, blue, red, blue. Add blue. Op red, blue, red. St bgrd. Bgrd and red in same hole. Drop bgrd. Cl red, blue, red, blue. Add blue. Op red, blue, red. St bgrd. Cl 3 bgrd.

Row 9. Op 3 bgrd. Cl red, blue, red, blue. Add gold. Op blue, red, blue, red. Drop st bgrd. St red. Cl blue, red, blue. Add gold. Op blue, red, blue, red. Drop st bgrd. Op 3 bgrd.

Row 10. Cl 2 bgrd to where bgrd and red in same hole. Drop bgrd. Cl red, blue, red, blue, gold. Add gold. Op blue, red, blue. St red. Drop st red. Cl blue, red, blue, gold. Add gold. Op blue, red, blue, red. St bgrd. Cl 2 bgrd.

Row 11. Op 2 bgrd. Add bgrd. Op red, blue, red, blue. St gold. Cl gold, blue, red, blue. Drop st red. Add gold. Op blue, red, blue. St gold. Cl gold, blue, red, blue, red. Drop st bgrd. Add bgrd. Op 2 bgrd.

Row 12. Cl 1 bgrd to where 2 bgrd in same hole. Cl 1 bgrd; op 1 bgrd. Op red, blue, red, blue. Drop st gold. St gold. Cl blue, red, blue, gold. Add gold. Op blue, red, blue. Drop st gold. St gold. Cl blue, red, blue, red. Cl 3 bgrd.

Row 13. Op 3 bgrd. Add bgrd. Op red, blue, red, blue. Drop st gold. St blue. Cl red, blue, gold. Add blue. Op gold, blue, red, blue. Drop st gold. St blue. Cl red, blue, red. Add bgrd. Op 3 bgrd.

Row 14. Cl 2 bgrd to where 2 bgrd in same hole. Cl 1 bgrd; op 1 bgrd. Op red, blue, red. St blue. Drop st blue. Cl red, blue, gold, blue. Add blue. Op gold, blue, red. St blue. Drop st blue. Cl red, blue, red. Cl 4 bgrd.

Row 15. Op 4 bgrd. Add bgrd. Op red, blue, red. Drop st blue. St red. Cl blue, gold, blue. Add red. Op blue, gold, blue, red. Drop st blue. St red. Cl blue, red. Add bgrd. Op 4 bgrd.

Row 16. Cl 3 bgrd to where 2 bgrd in same hole. Cl 1 bgrd; op 1 bgrd. Op red, blue. St red. Drop st red. Cl blue, gold, blue, red. Add red. Op blue, gold, blue. St red. Drop st red. Cl blue, red. Cl 5 bgrd.

Row 17. Op 5 bgrd. Add bgrd. Op red, blue. Drop st red. St blue. Cl gold, blue, red. Add blue. Op red, blue, gold, blue. Drop st red. St blue. Cl red. Add bgrd. Op 5 bgrd.

Row 18. Cl 4 bgrd to where 2 bgrd in same hole. Cl 1 bgrd; op 1 bgrd. Op red. St blue. Drop st blue. Cl gold, blue, red, blue. Add blue. Op red, blue, gold. St blue. Drop st blue. Cl red. Cl 6 bgrd.

Row 19. Op 6 bgrd. Add bgrd. Op red. Drop st blue. Op gold, blue, red. St blue. Cl blue, red, blue, gold. Drop st blue. Cl red. Add bgrd. Op 6 bgrd.

Row 20. Cl 5 bgrd to where 2 bgrd in same hole. Cl 1 bgrd; op 1 bgrd. Op red, gold, blue, red. Drop st blue. St blue. Cl red, blue, gold, red. Cl 7 bgrd.

Row 21. Op 7 bgrd. Add bgrd. Op red, gold, blue, red. Drop st blue. St red. Cl blue, gold, red. Add bgrd. Op 7 bgrd.

Row 22. Cl 6 bgrd to where 2 bgrd in same hole. Cl 1 bgrd; op 1 bgrd. Op red, gold, blue. St red. Drop st red. Cl blue, gold, red. Cl 8 bgrd.

Row 23. Op 8 bgrd. Add bgrd. Op red, gold, blue. Drop st red. St blue. Cl gold, red. Add bgrd. Op 8 bgrd.

Row 24. Cl 7 bgrd to where 2 bgrd in same hole. Cl 1 bgrd; op 1 bgrd. Op red, gold. St blue. Drop st blue. Cl gold, red. Cl 9 bgrd.

Row 25. Op 9 bgrd. Add bgrd. Op red, gold. Drop st blue. St gold. Cl red. Add bgrd. Op 9 bgrd.

Row 26. Cl 8 bgrd to where 2 bgrd in same hole. Cl 1 bgrd; op 1 bgrd. Op red. St gold. Drop st gold. Cl red. Cl 10 bgrd.

Row 27. Op 10 bgrd. Add bgrd. Op red. Drop st gold. St red. Add bgrd. Op 10 bgrd.

Row 28. Cl 9 bgrd to where 2 bgrd in same hole. Cl 1 bgrd; op 1 bgrd. St red. Drop st red. Cl 11 bgrd.

Row 29. Op 11 bgrd. Drop st red. Op 11 bgrd.

Pattern #103

Row	Pattern
1	x x x x 7 x x x / x x x 7 x x x
2	B
3	B B x x x 6 x x
4	B R B
5	B R R B x x 5 x x
6	B R G R B
7	B R G G R B x x 4 x x
8	B R G B G R B
9	B R G B B G R B x 3 x
10	B R G B R B G R B
11	B R G B R R B G R B x 2 x
12	B R G B R B G R B
13	B R G B B G R B x x 3 x
14	B R G B R B G R B
15	B R G B R R B G R B x 2 x
16	B R G B R G R B G R B
17	B R G B R G G R B G R B x
18	B R G B R G R G R B G R B
19	B R G B R G R R G R B G R B
20	B R G B R G R G R B G R B
21	B R G B R G G R B G R B x
22	B R G B R G R B G R B
23	B R G B R R B G R B x 2 x
24	B R G B R B G R B
25	B R G B B G R B x x 3 x
26	B R G B R B G R B
27	B R G B R R B G R B x 2 x
28	B R G B R B G R B
29	B R G B B G R B x x 3 x
30	B R G B G R B
31	B R G G R B x x x 4 x
32	B R G R B
33	B R R B x x x x 5 x
34	B R B
35	B B x x x x x 6 x
36	B
37	x x x x 7 x x x / x x x 7 x x x

R = Red
B = Blue
G = Green

Directions for Pattern #103

Note: Add bgrd in these directions means to add one background pull. *Drop bgrd* in directions means to drop one background pull. *St bgrd* means to stand one background pull.

Row 1. Op 7 bgrd. Add blue. Op 7 bgrd.

Row 2. Cl 6 bgrd to where bgrd and blue are in same hole. Drop bgrd. Cl blue. Add blue. St bgrd. Cl 6 bgrd.

Row 3. Op 6 bgrd. Cl blue. Add red. Op blue. Drop st bgrd. Op 6 bgrd.

Row 4. Cl 5 bgrd to where bgrd and blue are in same hole. Drop bgrd. Cl blue, red. Add red. Op blue. St bgrd. Cl 5 bgrd.

Row 5. Op 5 bgrd. Cl blue, red. Add green. Op red, blue. Drop st bgrd. Op 5 bgrd.

Row 6. Cl 4 bgrd to where bgrd and blue are in same hole. Drop bgrd. Cl blue, red, green. Add green. Op red, blue. St bgrd. Cl 4 bgrd.

Row 7. Op 4 bgrd. Cl blue, red, green. Add blue. Op green, red, blue. Drop st bgrd. Op 4 bgrd.

Row 8. Cl 3 bgrd to where bgrd and blue are in same hole. Drop bgrd. Cl blue, red, green, blue. Add blue. Op green, red, blue. St bgrd. Cl 3 bgrd.

Row 9. Op 3 bgrd. Cl blue, red, green, blue. Add red. Op blue, green, red, blue. Drop st bgrd. Op 3 bgrd.

Row 10. Cl 2 bgrd to where bgrd and blue are in same hole. Drop bgrd. Cl blue, red, green, blue, red. Add red. Op blue, green, red, blue. St bgrd. Cl 2 bgrd.

Row 11. Op 2 bgrd. Add bgrd. Op blue, red, green, blue. St red. Cl red, blue, green, red, blue. Drop st bgrd. Add bgrd. Op 2 bgrd.

Row 12. Cl 1 bgrd to where 2 bgrd in same hole. Cl 1 bgrd; op 1 bgrd. Op blue, red, green, blue. Drop st red. St red. Cl blue, green, red, blue. Cl 3 bgrd.

Row 13. Op 3 bgrd. Cl blue, red, green, blue. Drop st red. Add red. Op blue, green, red, blue. Op 3 bgrd.

Row 14. Cl 2 bgrd to where bgrd and blue are in same hole. Drop bgrd. Cl blue, red, green, blue, red. Add red. Op blue, green, red, blue. St bgrd. Cl 2 bgrd.

Row 15. Op 2 bgrd. Cl blue, red, green blue, red. Add green. Op red, blue, green, red, blue. Drop st bgrd. Op 2 bgrd.

Row 16. Cl 1 bgrd to where bgrd and blue are in same hole. Drop bgrd. Cl blue, red, green, blue, red, green. Add green. Op red, blue, green, red, blue. St bgrd. Cl 1 bgrd.

Row 17. Op 1 bgrd. Cl blue, red, green, blue, red, green. Add red. Op green, red, blue, green, red, blue. Drop st bgrd. Op 1 bgrd.

Row 18. Bgrd and blue in same hole. Drop bgrd. Cl blue, red, green, blue, red, green, red. Add red. Op green, red, blue, green, red, blue. St bgrd.

Row 19. Add bgrd. Op blue, red, green, blue, red, green. St red. Cl red, green, red, blue, green, red, blue. Drop st bgrd. Add bgrd.

Row 20. Bgrd and blue in same hole. Cl bgrd. Op blue, red, green, blue, red, green. Drop st red. St red. Cl green, red, blue, green, red, blue. Cl bgrd.

Row 21. Op 1 bgrd. Add bgrd. Op blue, red, green, blue, red, green. Drop st red. St green. Cl red, blue, green, red, blue. Add bgrd. Op 1 bgrd.

Row 22. 2 bgrd same hole. Cl 1 bgrd; op 1 bgrd. Op blue, red, green, blue, red. St green. Drop st green. Cl red, blue, green, red, blue. Cl 2 bgrd.

Row 23. Op 2 bgrd. Add bgrd. Op blue, red, green, blue, red. Drop st green. St red. Cl blue, green, red, blue. Add bgrd. Op 2 bgrd.

Row 24. Cl 1 bgrd to where 2 bgrd same hole. Cl 1 bgrd; op 1 bgrd. Op blue, red, green, blue. St red. Drop st red. Cl blue, green, red, blue. Cl 3 bgrd.

Row 25. Op 3 bgrd. Cl blue, red, green, blue. Drop st red. Add red. Op blue, green, red, blue. Op 3 bgrd.

Row 26. Cl 2 bgrd to where bgrd and blue are in same hole. Drop bgrd. Cl blue, red, green, blue, red. Add red. Op blue, green, red, blue. St bgrd. Cl 2 bgrd.

Row 27. Op 2 bgrd. Add bgrd. Op blue, red, green, blue. St red. Cl red, blue, green, red, blue. Drop st bgrd. Add bgrd. Op 2 bgrd.

Row 28. Cl 1 bgrd to where 2 bgrd same hole. Cl 1 bgrd; op 1 bgrd. Op blue, red, green, blue. Drop st red. St red. Cl blue, green, red, blue. Cl 3 bgrd.

Row 29. Op 3 bgrd. Add bgrd. Op blue, red, green, blue. Drop st red. St blue. Cl green,, red, blue. Add bgrd. Op 3 bgrd.

Row 30. Cl 2 bgrd to where 2 bgrd same hole. Cl 1 bgrd; op 1 bgrd. Op blue, red, green. St blue. Drop st blue. Cl green, red, blue. Cl 4 bgrd.

Row 31. Op 4 bgrd. Add bgrd. Op blue, red, green. Drop st blue. St green. Cl red, blue. Add bgrd. Op 4 bgrd.

Row 32. Cl 3 bgrd to where 2 bgrd same hole. Cl 1 bgrd; op 1 bgrd. Op blue, red. St green. Drop st green. Cl red, blue. Cl 5 bgrd.

Row 33. Op 5 bgrd. Add bgrd. Op blue, red. Drop st green. St red. Cl blue. Add bgrd. Op 5 bgrd.

Row 34. Cl 4 bgrd to where 2 bgrd same hole. Cl 1 bgrd; op 1 bgrd. Op blue. St red. Drop st red. Cl blue. Cl 6 bgrd.

Row 35. Op 6 bgrd. Add bgrd. Op blue. Drop st red. St blue. Add bgrd. Op 6 bgrd.

Row 36. Cl 5 bgrd to where 2 bgrd same hole. Cl 1 bgrd; op 1 bgrd. St blue. Drop st blue. Cl 7 bgrd.

Row 37. Op 7 bgrd. Drop st blue. Op 7 bgrd.

Pattern #104

```
 *  *  *  *7 *  *  */ *  *  *  *7 *  *     1  op
                   B                         2  cl
                   B  B  *  *  *  *6 *  *   3  op
                B  G  B                      4  cl
                B  G  G  B  *  *  *5 *      5  op
                B  G  R  G  B                6  cl
 *3 *  */ *  B  G  R  R  G  B  */ *  *3 *   7  op
       R  *  B  G  R  G  B  *  R             8  cl
       R  R  *  B  G  G  B  *  R  R  *2 *   9  op
    R  B  R  *  B  G  B  *  R  B  R         10  cl
    R  B  B  R  *  B  B  *  R  B  B  R  *   11  op
    R  G  B  B  R  *  B  *  R  B  B  G  R   12  cl
 R  G  G  B  B  R  *  *  R  B  B  G  G  R   13  op
    R  G  G  B  R  *  B  *  R  B  G  G  R   14  cl
    R  G  G  R  *  B  G  *  R  G  G  R  *   15  op
       R  G  R  *  B  G  B  *  R  G  R      16  cl
       R  R  *  B  G  G  B  *  R  R  *2 *   17  op
          R  *  B  G  R  G  B  *  R         18  cl
 *3 *  */ *  B  G  R  R  G  B  */ *  *3 *  19  op
                B  G  R  G  B                20  cl
                B  G  G  B  *  *  *  *5 *   21  op
                   B  G  B                   22  cl
                   B  B  *  *  *  *6 *  *   23  op
                      B                      24  cl
 *  *  *  *  *7 *  */ *  *  *  *  *7 *      25  op
```

R = Red
B = Blue
G = Green

Directions for Pattern #104

Note: Add Bgrd in these directions means to add one background pull. *Drop bgrd* in directions means to drop one background pull. *St bgrd* means to stand one background pull.

Row 1. Op 7 bgrd. Add blue. Op 7 bgrd.

Row 2. Cl 6 bgrd to where bgrd and blue in same hole. Drop bgrd. Cl blue. Add blue. St bgrd. Cl 6 bgrd.

Row 3. Op 6 bgrd. Cl blue. Add green. Op blue. Drop st bgrd. Op 6 bgrd.

Row 4. Cl 5 bgrd to where bgrd and blue in same hole. Drop bgrd. Cl blue, green. Add green. Op blue. St bgrd. Cl 5 bgrd.

Row 5. Op 5 bgrd. Cl blue, green. Add red. Op green, blue. Drop st bgrd. Op 5 bgrd.

Row 6. Cl 4 bgrd to where bgrd and blue in same hole. Drop bgrd. Cl blue, green, red. Add red. Op green, blue. St bgrd. Cl 4 bgrd.

Row 7. Op 3 bgrd. Add red. Op bgrd, blue, green. St red. Cl red, green, blue. Drop st bgrd. Cl bgrd. Add red. Op 3 bgrd.

Row 8. Cl 2 bgrd to where bgrd and red in same hole. Drop bgrd. Cl red. Add red. Op bgrd, blue, green. Drop st red. St red. Cl green, blue, bgrd, red. Add red. St bgrd. Cl 2 bgrd.

Row 9. Op 2 bgrd. Cl red. Add blue. Op red, bgrd, blue, green. Drop st red. St green. Cl blue, bgrd, red. Add blue. Op red. Drop st bgrd. Op 2 bgrd.

Row 10. Cl 1 bgrd to where bgrd and red in same hole. Drop bgrd. Cl red. Add blue. Op blue, red, bgrd, blue. St green. Drop st green. Cl blue, bgrd, red, blue. Add blue. Op red. St bgrd. Op 1 bgrd.

Row 11. Op 1 bgrd. Cl red. Add green. Op blue, blue, red, bgrd, blue. Drop st green. St blue. Cl bgrd, red, blue, blue. Add green. Op red. Drop st bgrd. Op 1 bgrd.

Row 12. Bgrd and red in same hole. Drop bgrd. Cl red. Add green. Op green, blue, blue, red, bgrd. St blue. Drop st blue. Cl bgrd, red, blue, blue, green. Add green. Op red. St bgrd.

Row 13. Add bgrd. Op red, green, green, blue. St blue. Cl red, bgrd. Drop st blue. Add blue. Op bgrd, red. St blue. Cl blue, green, green, red. Drop st bgrd. Add bgrd.

Row 14. Bgrd and red in same hole. Cl bgrd. Op red, green, green. St blue. Drop st blue. Cl red, bgrd, blue. Add blue. Op bgrd, red. Drop st blue. St blue. Cl green, green, red. Cl 1 bgrd.

Row 15. Op 1 bgrd. Add bgrd. Op red, green. St green. Drop st blue. Cl red, bgrd, blue. Add green. Op blue, bgrd, red. Drop st blue. St green. Cl green, red. Add bgrd. Op 1 bgrd.

Row 16. 2 bgrd in same hole. Cl 1 bgrd; op 1 bgrd. Op red. St green. Drop st green. Cl red, bgrd, blue, green. Add green. Op blue, bgrd, red. Drop st green. St green. Cl red. Cl 2 bgrd.

Row 17. Op 2 bgrd. Add bgrd. Op red. Drop st green. St red. Cl bgrd, blue, green. Add red. Op green, blue, bgrd, red. Drop st green. St red. Add bgrd. Op 2 bgrd.

Row 18. Cl 1 bgrd to where 2 bgrd in same hole. Cl 1 bgrd; op 1 bgrd. St red. Drop st red. Cl bgrd, blue, green, red. Add red. Op green, blue, bgrd. St red. Drop st red. Cl 3 bgrd.

Row 19. Op 3 bgrd. Drop st red. Op 1 bgrd. Add bgrd. Op blue, green. St red. Cl red, green, blue. Add bgrd. Op 1 bgrd. Drop st red. Op 3 bgrd.

Row 20. Cl 3 bgrd to where 2 bgrd in same hole. Cl 1 bgrd; op 1 bgrd. Op blue, green. Drop st red. St red. Cl green, blue. Cl 5 bgrd.

Row 21. Op 5 bgrd. Add bgrd. Op blue, green. Drop st red. St green. Cl blue. Add bgrd. Op 5 bgrd.

Row 22. Cl 4 bgrd to where 2 bgrd in same hole. Cl 1 bgrd; op 1 bgrd. Op blue. St green. Drop st green. Cl blue. Cl 6 bgrd.

Row 23. Op 6 bgrd. Add bgrd. Op blue. Drop st green. St blue. Add bgrd. Op 6 bgrd.

Row 24. Cl 5 bgrd to where 2 bgrd in same hole. Cl 1 bgrd; op 1 bgrd. St blue. Drop st blue. Cl 7 bgrd.

Row 25. Op 7 bgrd. Drop st blue. Op 7 bgrd.

Chapter 20: Complete Patterns and Directions

Pattern #105

Row	Pattern	#	Dir
1	x x x x7x x x/x x x7x x x x	1	op
2	R	2	cl
3	R R x x x x6x x	3	op
4	R G R	4	cl
5	R G G R x x x5x x	5	op
6	R R G R R	6	cl
7	R R B R R x x4x x	7	op
8	R R B R B R R	8	cl
9	R R B R R B R R x x3x	9	op
10	R R B B R B B R R	10	cl
11	R R B B G G B R R x2x	11	op
12	R R B B G R G B B R R	12	cl
13	R R B B G R R G B B R R x	13	op
14	R R B B G R R R G B B R R	14	cl
15	R R B B G R R R R G B B R R	15	op
16	R R B B G R R G B B R R	16	cl
17	R R B B G R R G B B R R x	17	op
18	R R B B G R G B B R R	18	cl
19	R R B B G G B R R x2x	19	op
20	R R B B R B B R R	20	cl
21	R R B R R B R R x x3x	21	op
22	R R B R B R R	22	cl
23	R R B R R x x4x	23	op
24	R R G R R	24	cl
25	R G G R x x x x5x	25	op
26	R G R	26	cl
27	R R x x x x6x x	27	op
28	R	28	cl
29	x x x x7x x/x x x x7x x x	29	op

R = Red
B = Blue
G = Gold

Directions for Pattern #105

Note: Add bgrd in these directions means to add one background pull. *Drop bgrd* in directions means to drop one background pull. *St bgrd* mans to stand one background pull.

Row 1. Op 7 bgrd. Add red. Op 7 bgrd.

Row 2. Cl 6 bgrd to where bgrd and red are in same hole Drop bgrd. Cl red. Add red. St bgrd. Cl 6 bgrd.

Row 3. Op 6 bgrd. Cl red. Add gold. Op red. Drop st bgrd. Op 6 bgrd.

Row 4. Cl 5 bgrd to where bgrd and red are in same hole. Drop bgrd. Cl red, gold. Add gold. Op red. St bgrd. Cl 5 bgrd.

Row 5. Op 5 bgrd. Cl red. Add red. St gold. Cl gold. Add red. Op red. Drop st bgrd. Op 5 bgrd.

Row 6. Cl 4 bgrd to where bgrd and red are in same hole. Drop bgrd. Cl red, red. Drop st gold. Add blue. St gold. Add blue. Op red, red. St bgrd. Cl 4 bgrd.

Row 7. Op 4 bgrd. Cl red, red, blue. Drop st gold. Add red. Op blue, red, red. Drop st bgrd. Op 4 bgrd.

Row 8. Cl 3 bgrd to where bgrd and red are in same hole. Drop bgrd. Cl red, red, blue, red. Add red. Op blue, red, red. St bgrd. Cl 3 bgrd.

Row 9. Op 3 bgrd. Cl red, red, blue. Add blue. St red. Cl red. Add blue. Op blue, red, red. Drop st bgrd. Op 3 bgrd.

Row 10. Cl 2 bgrd to where bgrd and red are in same hole. Drop bgrd. Cl red, red, blue, blue. Drop st red. Add gold. St red. Add gold. Op blue, blue, red, red. St bgrd. Cl 2 bgrd.

Row 11. Op 2 bgrd. Cl red, red, blue, blue, gold. Drop st red. Add red. Op gold, blue, blue, red, red. Drop st bgrd. Op 2 bgrd.

Row 12. Cl 1 bgrd to where bgrd and red are in same hole. Drop bgrd. Cl red, red, blue, blue, gold, red. Add red. Op gold, blue, blue, red, red. St bgrd. Cl 1 bgrd.

Row 13. Op 1 bgrd. Cl red, red, blue, blue, gold, red. Add red. Op red, gold, blue, blue, red, red. Drop st bgrd. Op 1 bgrd.

Row 14. Bgrd and red in same hole. Drop bgrd. Cl red, red, blue, blue, gold, red, red. Add red. Op red, gold, blue, blue, red, red. St bgrd.

Row 15. Add bgrd. Op red, red, blue, blue, gold, red. St red. Cl red, red, gold, blue, blue, red, red, Drop st bgrd. Add bgrd.

Row 16. Bgrd and red in same hole. Cl bgrd. Op red, red, blue, blue, gold, red. Drop st red. St red. Cl red, gold, blue, blue, red, red. Cl 1 bgrd.

Row 17. Op 1 bgrd. Add bgrd. Op red, red, blue, blue, gold, red. Drop st red. St red. Cl gold, blue, blue, red, red. Add bgrd. Op 1 bgrd.

Row 18. 2 bgrd in same hole. Cl 1 bgrd; op 1 bgrd. Op red, red, blue, blue, gold. St red. Drop st red. Cl gold, blue, blue, red, red. Cl 2 bgrd.

Row 19. Op 2 bgrd. Add bgrd. Op red, red, blue, blue. St gold. Drop st red. Add red. St gold. Cl blue, blue, red, red. Add bgrd. Op 2 bgrd.

Row 20. Cl 1 bgrd to where 2 bgrd in same hole Cl 1 bgrd; op 1 bgrd. Op red, red, blue. St blue. Drop st gold. Cl red. Drop st gold. Add red. St blue. Cl blue, red, red. Cl 3 bgrd.

Row 21. Op 3 bgrd. Add bgrd. Op red, red, blue. Drop st blue. St red. Cl red. Drop st blue. Cl blue, red, red. Add bgrd. Op 3 bgrd.

Row 22. Cl 2 bgrd to where 2 bgrd in same hole. Cl 1 bgrd; op 1 bgrd. Op red, red, blue. Drop st red. St red. Cl blue, red, red. Cl 4 bgrd.

Row 23. Op 4 bgrd. Add bgrd. Op red, red. St blue. Drop st red. Add gold. St blue. Cl red, red. Add bgrd. Op 4 bgrd.

Row 24. Cl 3 bgrd to where 2 bgrd in same hole. Cl 1 bgrd; op 1 bgrd. Op red. St red. Drop st blue. Cl gold. Drop st blue. Add gold. St red. Cl red. Cl 5 bgrd.

Row 25. Op 5 bgrd. Add bgrd. Op red. Drop st red. St gold. Cl gold. Drop st red. Cl red. Add bgrd. Op 5 bgrd.

Row 26. Cl 4 bgrd to where 2 bgrd in same hole. Cl 1 bgrd; op 1 bgrd. Op red. Drop st gold. St gold. Cl red. Cl 6 bgrd.

Row 27. Op 6 bgrd. Add bgrd. Op red. Drop st gold. St red. Add bgrd. Op 6 bgrd.

Row 28. Cl 5 bgrd to where 2 bgrd in same hole. Cl 1 bgrd; op 1 bgrd. St red. Drop st red. Cl 7 bgrd.

Row 29. Op 7 bgrd. Drop st red. Op 7 bgrd.

Pattern #106

/	*	*	*	*	*	*	*12*	*	*	*	*/*		1	op
R	-	-	-	-	-	-	-11-	-	-	-	R		2	cl
R	*	*	*5*	*	/*	*	-	*5*	R	*			3	op
R	-	*4*	-	-	B	-	-	*4*	-	R			4	cl
R	*	*3*	B	B	*	-	*3*	R	*2*				5	op
R	-	*2*	B	G	B	-	*2*	R					6	cl
R	*	B	G	G	B	*	R	*	*3*				7	op
R	B	G	R	G	B	R							8	cl
R	G	R	R	G	R	*	-	*4*					9	op
G	R	G	R	G	R	G							10	cl
G	B	R	G	G	R	B	G	*	*3*				11	op
G	B	R	R	G	R	R	B	G					12	cl
G	B	R	G	R	R	G	R	B	G	*2*			13	op
G	B	R	G	B	R	B	G	R	B	G			14	cl
G	B	R	G	B	B	B	B	G	R	B	G	*	15	op
G	B	R	G	B	R	B	G	R	B	G			16	cl
G	B	R	G	R	R	G	R	B	G	*2*			17	op
G	B	R	R	G	R	R	B	G					18	cl
G	B	R	G	G	R	B	G	*	*3*				19	op
G	R	G	R	G	R	G							20	cl
R	G	R	R	G	R	*	-	*4*					21	op
R	B	G	R	G	B	R							22	cl
R	*	B	G	G	B	*	R	*	*3*				23	op
R	*	*2*	B	G	B	*	*2*	R					24	cl
R	*	*3*	B	B	*	*3*	R						25	op
R	-	*4*	-	B	-	-	*4*	-	R				26	cl
R	*	*	*5*	*	*/*	*	*	*5*	R				27	op
R	-	-	-	-	-	*11*	-	-	-	-	R		28	cl
/	*	*	*	-	*12*	-	-	-	*	*/*			29	op

R = Red
B = Blue
G = Green

Directions for Pattern #106

Note: Add bgrd in these directions means to add one background pull. *Drop bgrd* in directions means to drop one background pull. *St bgrd* means to stand one background pull.

Row 1. Op 1 bgrd. Add red. Op 12 bgrd. Add red. Op bgrd.

Row 2. Bgrd and red in same hole. Cl bgrd. Op red. St bgrd. Cl 10 bgrd to where bgrd and red in same hole. Drop bgrd. Cl red. Cl bgrd.

Row 3. Op 1 bgrd. Add bgrd. Op red. Drop st bgrd. Op 5 bgrd. Add blue. Op 5 bgrd. Cl red. Add bgrd. Op 1 bgrd.

Row 4. 2 bgrd in same hole. Cl 1 bgrd; op 1 bgrd. Op red. St bgrd. Cl 3 bgrd to where bgrd and blue in same hole. Drop bgrd. Cl blue. Add blue. St bgrd. Cl 3 bgrd to where bgrd and red in same hole. Drop bgrd. Cl red. Cl 2 bgrd.

Row 5. Op 2 bgrd. Add bgrd. Op red. Drop st bgrd. Op 3 bgrd. Cl blue. Add green. Op blue. Drop st bgrd. Op 3 bgrd. Cl red. Add bgrd. Op 2 bgrd.

Row 6. Cl 1 bgrd to where 2 bgrd in same hole Cl 1 bgrd; op 1 bgrd. Op red. St bgrd. Cl 1 bgrd. Bgrd and blue in same hole. Drop bgrd. Cl blue, green. Add green. Op blue. St bgrd. Cl 1 bgrd. Bgrd and red in same hole. Drop bgrd. Cl red. Cl 3 bgrd.

Row 7. Op 3 bgrd. Add bgrd. Op red. Drop st bgrd. St bgrd. Cl blue, green. Add red. Op green, blue. Drop st bgrd. St bgrd. Cl red. Add bgrd. Op 3 bgrd.

Row 8. Cl 2 bgrd to where 2 bgrd in same hole. Cl 1 bgrd; op 1 bgrd. Op red. Drop st bgrd. St blue. Cl green, red. Add red. Op green. St blue. Drop st bgrd. Cl red. Cl 4 bgrd.

Row 9. Op 4 bgrd. Add green. Op red. Drop st blue. Op green. St red. Cl red, green. Drop st blue. Cl red. Add green. Op 4 bgrd.

Row 10. Cl 3 bgrd to where bgrd and green in same hole. Drop bgrd. Cl green. Add blue. Op red, green. Drop st red. St red. Cl green, red. Add blue. Op green. St bgrd. Cl 3 bgrd.

Row 11. Cl 3 bgrd. Cl green, blue. Add red. Op red, green. Drop st red. St green. Cl red. Add red. Op blue, green. Drop st bgrd. Op 3 bgrd.

Row 12. Cl 2 bgrd to where bgrd and green in same hole. Drop bgrd. Cl green, blue, red. Add green. Op red. St green. Drop st green. Cl red. Add green. Op red, blue, green. St bgrd. Cl 2 bgrd.

Row 13. Op 2 bgrd. Cl green, blue, red, green. Add blue. Op red. Drop st green. St red. Add blue. Op green, red, blue, green. Drop st bgrd. Op 2 bgrd.

Row 14. Cl 1 bgrd to where bgrd and green in same hole. Drop bgrd. Cl green, blue, red, green, blue. Add blue. St red. Drop st red. Cl blue. Add blue. Op green, red, blue, green. St bgrd. Cl 1 bgrd.

Row 15. Op 1 bgrd. Add bgrd. Op green, blue, red, green. St blue. Cl blue. Drop st red. Add red. St blue. Cl blue, green, red, blue, green. Drop st bgrd. Add bgrd. Op 1 bgrd.

Row 16. 2 bgrd in same hole. Cl 1 bgrd; op 1 bgrd. Op green, blue, red, green. Drop st blue. St blue. Cl red. Add red. Drop st blue. St blue. Cl green, red, blue, green. Cl 2 bgrd.

Row 17. Op 2 bgrd. Add bgrd. Op green, blue, red. St green. Drop st blue. Cl red. Add green. Op red. Drop st blue. St green. Cl red, blue, green. Add bgrd. Op 2 bgrd.

Row 18. Cl 1 bgrd to 2 bgrd in same hole. Cl 1 bgrd; op 1 bgrd. Op green, blue. St red. Drop st green. Cl red, green. Add green. Op red. Drop st green. St red. Cl blue, green. Cl 3 bgrd.

Row 19. Op 3 bgrd. Add bgrd. Op green. St blue. Drop st red. Cl red, green. Add red. Op green, red. Drop st red. St blue. Cl green. Add bgrd. Op 3 bgrd.

Row 20. Cl 2 bgrd to 2 bgrd in same hole. Cl 1 bgrd; op 1 bgrd. St green. Drop st blue. Cl red, green, red. Add red. Op green, red. Drop st blue. St green. Cl 4 bgrd.

Row 21. Op 4 bgrd. Drop st green. Cl red. Add blue. Op green. St red. Cl red, green. Add blue. Op red. Drop st green. Op 4 bgrd.

Row 22. Cl 3 bgrd to where bgrd and red are in same hole. Drop bgrd. Cl red. Add bgrd. Op blue, green. Drop st red. St red. Cl green, blue. Add bgrd. Op red. St bgrd. Cl 3 bgrd.

Row 23. Op 3 bgrd. Cl red. Add bgrd. Op 1 bgrd. Op blue, green. Drop st red. St green. Cl blue. Add bgrd. Op 1 bgrd. Op red. Drop st bgrd. Op 3 bgrd.

Row 24. Cl 2 bgrd to where bgrd and red are in same hole. Drop bgrd. Cl red. Cl 2 bgrd. Add bgrd. Op blue. St green. Drop st green. Cl blue. Cl 2 bgrd. Add bgrd. Op red. St bgrd. Cl 2 bgrd.

Row 25. Op 2 bgrd. Cl red. Add bgrd. Op 3 bgrd. Op blue. Drop st green. St blue. Add bgrd. Op 3 bgrd. Op red. Drop st bgrd. Op 2 bgrd.

Row 26. Cl 1 bgrd to where bgrd and red are in same hole. Drop bgrd. Cl red. Cl 4 bgrd. Add bgrd. St blue. Drop st blue. Cl 4 bgrd. Add bgrd. Op red. St bgrd. Cl 1 bgrd.

Row 27. Op 1 bgrd. Cl red. Add bgrd. Op 5 bgrd. Drop st blue. Op 5 bgrd. Op red. Drop st bgrd. Op 1 bgrd.

Row 28. Bgrd and red in same hole. Op bgrd. St red. Cl 11 bgrd. Add bgrd. St red. Cl bgrd.

Row 29. Op 1 bgrd. Drop st red. Op 12 bgrd. Drop st red. Op 1 bgrd.

Pattern #107

Row																	#	
*	*4*	*	/	*	*	*	*7*	*	*/*	*	*	*	*7*	*/	*	*4*	1	op
		B	*	*	*6*	*	*	R	*	*	*	*6*	*	*	B		2	cl
		B	B	*	*	*5*	*	R	R	*	*	*5*	B	B	*	*3*	3	op
		B	R	B	*	*4*	*	R	B	R	*	*4*	*	B	R	B	4	cl
		B	R	R	B	*	*3*	R	B	B	R	*	*3*	B	R	R	B	*2*	5	op
		B	R	G	R	B	*	*2*	R	B	G	B	R	*	*2*	B	R	G	R	B	6	cl
*	B	R	G	G	R	B	*	R	B	G	G	B	R	*	B	R	G	G	R	B	*	7	op
	B	R	G	R	B	*	R	B	G	B	G	B	R	*	B	R	G	R	B		8	cl
	B	R	R	B	*	R	B	G	B	B	G	B	R	*	B	R	R	B	*2*	9	op
		B	R	B	*	R	B	G	B	R	B	G	B	R	*	B	R	B		10	cl
		B	B	*	R	B	G	B	R	R	B	G	B	R	*	B	B	*	*3*	11	op
			B	*	R	B	G	B	R	B	R	B	G	B	R	*	B		12	cl
*	*4*	*/*	R	B	G	B	R	B	B	R	B	G	B	R	*/*	*	*4*	13	op
		B	*	R	B	G	B	R	B	R	B	G	B	R	*	B	14	cl
		B	B	*	R	B	G	B	R	R	B	G	B	R	*	B	B	*	*3*	15	op
		B	R	B	*	R	B	G	B	R	B	G	B	R	*	B	R	B	16	cl
		B	R	R	B	*	R	B	G	B	B	G	B	R	*	B	R	R	B	*2*	17	op
	B	R	G	R	B	*	R	B	G	B	G	B	R	*	B	R	G	R	B	18	cl
	B	R	G	G	R	B	*	R	B	G	G	B	R	*	B	R	G	G	R	B	*	19	op
		B	R	G	R	B	*	*2*	R	B	G	B	R	*	*2*	B	R	G	R	B	20	cl
		B	R	R	B	*	*3*	R	B	B	R	*	*3*	B	R	R	B	*2*	21	op
		B	R	B	*	*	*4*	*	R	B	R	*	*	*4*	*	B	R	B	22	cl
			B	B	*	*	*5*	*	R	R	*	*	*5*	B	B	*	*3*	23	op
			B	*	*	*6*	*	*	R	*	*	*6*	*	B		24	cl
*	*	*4*	*/*	*	*	*	*7*	*	*/	*	*	*	*7*	*/	*	*4*	*	25	op

R = Red
B = Blue
G = Gold

Directions for Pattern #107

Note: Add bgrd in these directions means to add one background pull. *Drop bgrd* in directions means to drop one background pull. *St bgrd* means to stand one background pull.

Row 1. Op 4 bgrd. Add blue. Op 7 bgrd. Add red. Op 7 bgrd. Add blue. Op 4 bgrd.

Row 2. Cl 3 bgrd to where bgrd and blue in same hole. Drop bgrd. Cl blue. Add blue. St bgrd. Cl 5 bgrd to where bgrd and red in same hole. Drop bgrd. Cl red. Add red. St bgrd. Cl 5 bgrd to where bgrd and blue in same hole. Drop bgrd. Cl blue. Add blue. St bgrd. Cl 3 bgrd.

Row 3. Op 3 bgrd. Cl blue. Add red. Op blue. Drop st bgrd. Op 5 bgrd. Cl red. Add blue. Op red. Drop st bgrd. Op 5 bgrd. Cl blue. Add red. Op blue. Drop st bgrd. Op 3 bgrd.

Row 4. Cl 2 bgrd to where bgrd and blue in same hole. Drop bgrd. Cl blue, red. Add red. Op blue. St bgrd. Cl 3 bgrd to where bgrd and red in same hole. Drop bgrd. Cl red, blue. Add blue. Op red. St bgrd. Cl 3 bgrd to where bgrd and blue in same hole. Drop bgrd. Cl blue, red. Add red. Op blue. St bgrd. Cl 2 blue.

Row 5. Op 2 bgrd. Cl blue, red. Add gold. Op red, blue. Drop st bgrd. Op 3 bgrd. Cl red, blue. Add gold. Op blue, red. Drop st bgrd. Op 3 bgrd. Cl blue, red. Add gold. Op red, blue. Drop st bgrd. Op 2 bgrd.

Row 6. Cl 1 bgrd to where bgrd and blue in same hole. Drop bgrd. Cl blue, red, gold. Add gold. Op red, blue. St bgrd. Cl 1 bgrd to where bgrd and red in same hole. Drop bgrd. Cl red, blue, gold. Add gold. Op blue, red. St bgrd. Cl 1 bgrd to where bgrd and blue in same hole. Drop bgrd. Cl blue, red, gold. Add gold. Op red, blue. St bgrd. Cl 1 bgrd.

Row 7. Op 1 bgrd. Add bgrd. Op blue, red. St gold. Cl gold, red, blue. Drop st bgrd. Cl bgrd, red, blue, gold. Add blue. Op gold, blue, red. Drop st bgrd. Op bgrd, blue, red. St gold. Cl gold, red, blue. Drop st bgrd. Add bgrd. Op 1 bgrd.

Row 8. 2 bgrd in same hole. Cl 1 bgrd; op 1 bgrd. Op blue, red. Drop st gold. St gold. Cl red, blue, bgrd, red, blue, gold, blue. Add blue. Op gold, blue, red, bgrd, blue, red. Drop st gold. St gold. Cl red, blue. Cl 2 bgrd.

Row 9. Op 2 bgrd. Add bgrd. Op blue, red. Drop st gold. St red. Cl blue, bgrd, red, blue, gold, blue. Add red. Op blue, gold, blue, red, bgrd, blue, red. Drop st gold. St red. Cl blue. Add bgrd. Op 2 bgrd.

Row 10. Cl 1 bgrd to where 2 bgrd in same hole. Cl 1 bgrd; op 1 bgrd. Op blue. St red. Drop st red. Cl blue, bgrd, red, blue, gold, blue, red. Add red. Op blue, gold, blue, red, bgrd, blue. St red. Drop st red. Cl blue. Cl 3 bgrd.

Row11. Op 3 bgrd Add bgrd. Op blue. Drop st red. St blue Cl bgrd, red, blue, gold, blue, red. Add blue. Op red, blue, gold, blue, red, bgrd, blue. Drop st red. St blue. Add bgrd. Op 3 bgrd.

Row 12. Cl 2 bgrd to where 2 bgrd in same hole. Cl 1 bgrd; op 1 bgrd. St blue. Drop st blue. Cl bgrd, red, blue, gold, blue, red, blue. Add blue. Op red, blue, gold, blue, red, bgrd. St blue. Drop st blue. Cl 4 bgrd.

Row 13. Op 4 bgrd. Drop st blue. Add blue. Op bgrd, red, blue, gold, blue, red. St blue. Cl blue, red, blue, gold, blue, red, bgrd. Drop st blue. Add blue. Op 4 bgrd.

Row 14. Cl 3 bgrd to where bgrd and blue in same hole. Drop bgrd. Cl blue. Add blue. Op bgrd, red, blue, gold, blue, red. Drop st blue. St blue. Cl red, blue, gold, blue, red, bgrd, blue. Add blue. St bgrd. Cl 3 bgrd.

Row 15. Op 3 bgrd. Cl blue. Add red. Op blue, bgrd, red, blue, gold, blue, red. Drop st blue. St red. Cl blue, gold, blue, red, bgrd, blue. Add red. Op blue. Drop st bgrd. Op 3 bgrd.

Row 16. Cl 2 bgrd to where bgrd and blue in same hole. Drop bgrd. Cl blue, red. Add red. Op blue, bgrd, red, blue, gold, blue. St red. Drop st red. Cl blue, gold, blue, red, bgrd, blue, red. Add red. Op blue. St bgrd. Cl 2 bgrd.

Row 17. Op 2 bgrd. Cl blue, red. Add gold. Op red, blue, bgrd, red, blue, gold, blue. Drop st red. St blue. Cl gold, blue, red, bgrd, blue, red. Add gold. Op red, blue. Drop st bgrd. Op 2 bgrd.

Row 18. Cl 1 bgrd to where bgrd and blue in same hole. Drop bgrd. Cl blue, red, gold. Add gold. Op red, blue, bgrd, red, blue, gold. St blue. Drop st blue. Cl gold, blue, red, bgrd, blue, red, gold. Add gold. Op red, blue. St bgrd. Cl 1 bgrd.

Row 19. Op 1 bgrd. Add bgrd. Op blue, red. St gold. Cl gold, red, blue. Add bgrd. Op bgrd, red, blue, gold. Drop st blue. St gold. Cl blue, red. Add bgrd. Op bgrd, blue, red. St gold. Cl gold, red, blue. Drop st bgrd. Add bgrd. Op 1 bgrd.

Row 20. 2 bgrd in same hole. Cl 1 bgrd; op 1 bgrd. Op blue, red. Drop st gold. St gold. Cl red, blue. Cl 2 bgrd. Add bgrd. Op red, blue. St gold. Drop st gold. Cl blue, red. Cl 2 bgrd. Add bgrd. Op blue, red. Drop st gold. St gold. Cl red, blue. Cl 2 bgrd.

Row 21. Op 2 bgrd. Add bgrd. Op blue, red. Drop st gold. St red. Cl blue. Add bgrd. Op 3 bgrd. Op red, blue. Drop st gold. St blue. Cl red. Add bgrd. Op 3 bgrd. Op blue, red. Drop st gold. St red. Cl blue. Add bgrd. Op 2 bgrd.

Row 22. Cl 1 bgrd to where 2 bgrd in same hole. Cl 1 bgrd; op 1 bgrd. Op blue. St red. Drop st red. Cl blue. Cl 4 bgrd. Add bgrd. Op red. St blue. Drop st blue. Cl red. Cl 4 bgrd. Add bgrd. Op blue. St red. Drop st red. Cl blue. Cl 3 bgrd.

Row 23. Op 3 bgrd. Add bgrd. Op blue. Drop st red. St blue. Add bgrd. Op 5 bgrd. Op red. Drop st blue. St red. Add bgrd. Op 5 bgrd. Op blue. Drop st red. St blue. Add bgrd. Op 3 bgrd.

Row 24. Cl 2 bgrd to where 2 bgrd in same hole. Cl 1 bgrd; op 1 bgrd. St blue. Drop st blue. Cl 6 bgrd. Add bgrd. St red. Drop st red. Cl 6 bgrd. Add bgrd. St blue. Drop st blue. Cl 4 bgrd.

Row 25. Op 4 bgrd. Drop st blue. Op 7 bgrd. Drop st red. Op 7 bgrd. Drop st blue. Op 4 bgrd.

Pattern #108

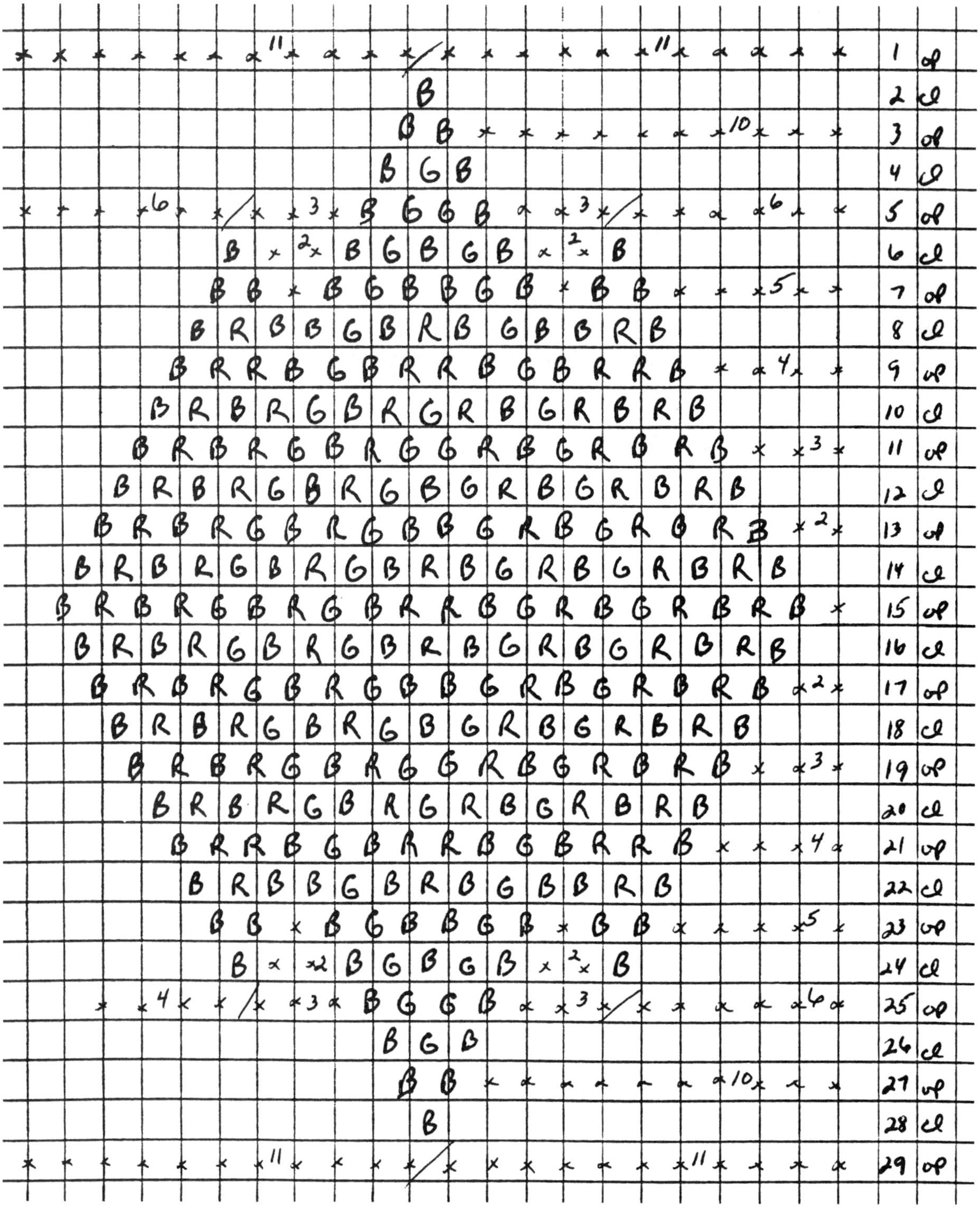

R= Red
B= Blue
G= Gold

Directions for Pattern #108

Note: Add Bgrd in these directions means to add one background pull. *Drop bgrd* in directions means to drop one background pull. *St bgrd* means to stand one background pull.

Row 1. Op 11 bgrd. Add blue. Op 11 bgrd.

Row 2. Cl 10 bgrd to where bgrd and blue in same hole. Drop bgrd. Cl blue. Add blue. St bgrd. Cl 10 bgrd.

Row 3. Op 10 bgrd. Cl blue. Add gold. Op blue. Drop st bgrd. Op 10 bgrd.

Row 4. Cl 9 bgrd to where bgrd and blue in same hole. Drop bgrd. Cl blue, gold. Add gold. Op blue. St bgrd. Cl 9 bgrd.

Row 5. Op 6 bgrd. Add blue. Op 3 bgrd. Cl blue, gold. Add blue. Op gold, blue. Drop st bgrd. Op 3 bgrd. Add blue. Op 6 bgrd.

Row 6. Cl 5 bgrd to where bgrd and blue in same hole. Drop bgrd. Cl blue. Add blue. St bgrd. Cl 1 bgrd to where bgrd and blue in same hole. Drop bgrd. Cl blue, gold, blue. Add blue. Op gold, blue. St bgrd. Cl 1 bgrd to where bgrd and blue in same hole. Drop bgrd. Cl blue. Add blue. St bgrd. Cl 5 bgrd.

Row 7. Op 5 bgrd. Cl blue. Add red. Op blue. Drop st bgrd. St bgrd. Cl blue, gold, blue. Add red. Op blue, gold, blue. Drop st bgrd. St bgrd. Cl blue. Add red. Op blue. Drop st bgrd. Op 5 bgrd.

Row 8. Cl 4 bgrd to where bgrd and blue in same hole. Drop bgrd. Cl blue, red. Add red. Op blue. Drop st bgrd. St blue. Cl gold, blue, red. Add red. Op blue, gold, blue. Drop st bgrd. St blue. Cl red. Add red. Op blue. St bgrd. Cl 4 bgrd.

Row 9. Op 4 bgrd. Cl blue, red. Add blue. Op red. St blue. Drop st blue. Cl gold, blue, red. Add gold. Op red, blue, gold. St blue. Drop st blue. Cl red. Add blue. Op red, blue. Drop st bgrd. Op 4 bgrd.

Row 10. Cl 3 bgrd to where bgrd and blue in same hole. Drop bgrd. Cl blue, red, blue, red. Drop st blue. Cl gold, blue, red, gold. Add gold. Op red, blue, gold. Drop st blue. Op red, blue, red, blue. St bgrd. Cl 3 bgrd.

Row 11. Op 3 bgrd. Cl blue, red, blue, red, gold, blue, red, gold. Add blue. Op gold, red, blue, gold, red, blue, red, blue. Drop st bgrd. Op 3 bgrd.

Row 12. Cl 2 bgrd to where bgrd and blue in same hole. Drop bgrd. Cl blue, red, blue, red, gold, blue, red, gold, blue. Add blue. Op gold, red, blue, gold, red, blue, red, blue. St bgrd. Cl 2 bgrd.

Row 13. Op 2 bgrd. Cl blue, red, blue, red, gold, blue, red, gold, blue. Add red. Op blue, gold, red, blue, gold, red, blue, red, blue. Drop st bgrd. Op 2 bgrd.

Row 14. Cl 1 bgrd to where bgrd and blue in same hole. Drop bgrd. Cl blue, red, blue, red, gold, blue, red, gold, blue, red. Add red. Op blue, gold, red, blue, gold, red, blue, red, blue. St bgrd. Cl 1 bgrd.

Row 15. Op 1 bgrd. Add bgrd. Op blue, red, blue, red, gold, blue, red, gold, blue. St red. Cl red, blue, gold, red, blue, gold, red, blue, red, blue. Drop st bgrd. Add bgrd. Op 1 bgrd.

Row 16. 2 bgrd in same hole. Cl 1 bgrd; op 1 bgrd. Op blue, red, blue, red, gold, blue, red, gold, blue. Drop st red. St red. Cl blue, gold, red, blue, gold, red, blue, red, blue. Cl 2 bgrd.

Row 17. Op 2 bgrd. Add bgrd. Op blue, red, blue, red, gold, blue, red, gold, blue. Drop st red. St blue. Cl gold, red, blue, gold, red, blue, red, blue. Add bgrd. Op 2 bgrd.

Row 18. Cl 1 bgrd to where 2 bgrd in same hole. Cl 1 bgrd; op 1 bgrd. Op blue, red, blue, red, gold, blue, red, gold. St blue. Drop st blue. Cl gold, red, blue, gold, red, blue, red, blue. Cl 3 bgrd.

Row 19. Op 3 bgrd. Add bgrd. Op blue, red, blue, red, gold, blue, red, gold. Drop st blue. St gold. Cl red, blue, gold, red, blue, red, blue. Add bgrd. Op 3 bgrd.

Row 20. Cl 2 bgrd to where 2 bgrd in same hole. Cl 1 bgrd; op 1 bgrd. Op blue, red. St blue. Cl red. Add blue. Op gold, blue, red. St gold. Drop st gold. Cl red, blue, gold. Add blue. Op red. St blue. Cl red, blue. Cl 4 bgrd.

Row 21. Op 4 bgrd. Add bgrd. Op blue, red. Drop st blue. St red. Cl blue. Add blue. Op gold, blue, red. Drop st gold. St red. Cl blue, gold, blue. Add blue. Op red. Drop st blue. St red. Cl blue. Add bgrd. Op 4 bgrd.

Row 22. Cl 3 bgrd to where 2 bgrd in same hole. Cl 1 bgrd; op 1 bgrd. Op blue. St red. Drop st red. Cl blue. Add bgrd. Op blue, gold, blue. St red. Drop st red. Cl blue, gold, blue. Add bgrd. Op blue. St red. Drop st red. Cl blue. Cl 5 bgrd.

Row 23. Op 5 bgrd. Add bgrd. Op blue. Drop st red. St blue. Add bgrd. Op 1 bgrd. Op blue, gold, blue. Drop st red. St blue. Cl gold, blue. Add bgrd. Op 1 bgrd. Op blue. Drop st red. St blue. Add bgrd. Op 5 bgrd.

Row 24. Cl 4 bgrd to where 2 bgrd in same hole. Cl 1 bgrd; op 1 bgrd. St blue. Drop st blue. Cl 2 bgrd. Add bgrd. Op blue, gold. St blue. Drop st blue. Cl gold, blue. Cl 2 bgrd. Add bgrd. St blue. Drop st blue. Cl 6 bgrd.

Row 25. Op 6 bgrd. Drop st blue. Op 3 bgrd. Add bgrd. Op blue, gold. Drop st blue. St gold. Cl blue. Add bgrd. Op 3 bgrd. Drop st blue. Op 6 bgrd.

Row 26. Cl 8 bgrd to where 2 bgrd in same hole. Cl 1 bgrd; op 1 bgrd. Op blue. St gold. Drop st gold. Cl blue. Cl 10 bgrd.

Row 27. Op 10 bgrd. Add bgrd. Op blue. Drop st gold. St blue. Add bgrd. Op 10 bgrd.

Row 28. Cl 9 bgrd to where 2 bgrd in same hole. Cl 1 bgrd; op 1 bgrd. St blue. Drop st blue. Cl 11 bgrd.

Row 29. Op 11 bgrd. Drop st blue. Op 11 bgrd.

Pattern #109

R = Red
B = Blue
G = Gold

Directions for Pattern #109

Note: Add bgrd in these directions means to add one background pull. *Drop bgrd* in directions means to drop one background pull. *St bgrd* means to stand one background pull.

Row 1. Op 2 bgrd. Add blue. Op 6 bgrd. Add blue. Op 6 bgrd. Add blue. Op 6 bgrd. Add blue. Op 2 bgrd.

Row 2. Cl 1 bgrd to where bgrd and blue in same hole. Drop bgrd. Cl blue. Add blue. St bgrd. Cl 4 bgrd to where bgrd and blue in same hole. Drop bgrd. Cl blue. Add blue. St bgrd. Cl 4 bgrd to where bgrd and blue in same hole. Drop bgrd. Cl blue. Add blue. St bgrd. Cl 4 bgrd to where bgrd and blue in same hole. Drop bgrd. Cl blue. Add blue. St bgrd. Cl 1 bgrd.

Row 3. Op 1 bgrd. Cl blue. Add gold. Op blue. Drop st bgrd. Op 4 bgrd. Cl blue. Add red. Op blue. Drop st bgrd. Op 4 bgrd. Cl blue. Add red. Op blue. Drop st bgrd. Op 4 bgrd. Cl blue. Add gold. Op blue. Drop st bgrd. Op 1 bgrd.

Row 4. Bgrd and blue in same hole. Drop bgrd. Cl blue. Add red. Op gold, blue. St bgrd. Cl 2 bgrd to where bgrd and blue in same hole. Drop bgrd. Cl blue, red. Add gold. Op blue. St bgrd. Cl 2 bgrd to where bgrd and blue in same hole. Drop bgrd. Cl blue. Add gold. Op red, blue. St bgrd. Cl 2 bgrd to where bgrd and blue in same hole. Drop bgrd. Cl blue, gold. Add red. Op blue. St bgrd.

Row 5. Add bgrd. Op blue, red, gold, blue. Drop st bgrd. Op 2 bgrd. Cl blue, red, gold. Add blue. Op blue. Drop st bgrd. Op 2 bgrd. Cl blue. Add blue. Op gold, red, blue. Drop st bgrd. Op 2 bgrd. Cl blue, gold, red, blue. Drop st bgrd. Add bgrd.

Row 6. Cl 1 bgrd. Op blue, red, gold, blue. St bgrd. Bgrd and blue in same hole. Drop bgrd. Cl blue, red, gold, blue. Add red. Op blue. St bgrd. Bgrd and blue in same hole. Drop bgrd. Cl blue. Add red. Op blue, gold, red, blue. St bgrd. Bgrd and blue in same hole. Drop bgrd. Cl blue, gold, red, blue. Cl 1 bgrd.

Row 7. Op 1 bgrd. Add bgrd. Op blue, red, gold, blue. Drop st bgrd. Op blue, red, gold, blue, red, blue. Drop st bgrd. St blue. Cl red, blue, gold, red, blue. Drop st bgrd. Cl blue, gold, red, blue. Add bgrd. Op 1 bgrd.

Row 8. 2 bgrd in same hole. Cl 1 bgrd; op 1 bgrd. Op blue, red, gold. St blue. Add red. Op blue, red, gold, blue, red. St blue. Drop st blue. Cl red, blue, gold, red, blue. Add red. St blue. Cl gold, red, blue. Cl 2 bgrd.

Row 9. Op 2 bgrd. Add bgrd. Op blue, red, gold. Drop st blue. Op red, blue, red, gold, blue, red. Drop st blue. St red. Cl blue, gold, red, blue, red. Drop st blue. Cl gold, red, blue. Add bgrd. Op 2 bgrd.

Row 10. Cl 1 bgrd to where 2 bgrd in same hole. Cl 1 bgrd; op 1 bgrd. Op blue, red, gold, red, blue, red, gold, blue. St red. Drop st red. Cl blue, gold, red, blue, red, gold, red, blue. Cl 3 bgrd.

Row 11. Op 3 bgrd. Add bgrd. Op blue, red, gold, red, blue, red, gold, blue. Drop st red. St blue. Cl gold, red, blue, red, gold, red, blue. Add bgrd. Op 3 bgrd.

Row 12. Cl 2 bgrd to where 2 bgrd in same hole. Cl 1 bgrd; op 1 bgrd. Op blue, red, gold, red, blue, red, gold. St blue. Drop st blue. Cl gold, red, blue, red, gold, red, blue. Cl 4 bgrd.

Row 13. Op 4 bgrd. Add bgrd. Op blue, red, gold, red, blue, red, gold. Drop st blue. St gold. Cl red, blue, red, gold, red, blue. Add bgrd. Op 4 bgrd.

Row 14. Cl 3 bgrd to where 2 bgrd in same hole. Cl 1 bgrd; op 1 bgrd. Op blue, red, gold, red, blue, red. St gold. Drop st gold. Cl red, blue, red, gold, red, blue. Cl 5 bgrd.

Row 15. Op 5 bgrd. Add bgrd. Op blue, red, gold, red, blue, red. Drop st gold. St red. Cl blue, red, gold, red, blue. Add bgrd. Op 5 bgrd.

Row 16. Cl 4 bgrd to where 2 bgrd in same hole. Cl 1 bgrd; op 1 bgrd. Op blue, red, gold, red, blue. St red. Drop st red. Cl blue, red, gold, red, blue. Cl 6 bgrd.

Row 17. Op 6 bgrd. Cl blue, red, gold, red, blue. Drop st red. Add red. Op blue, red, gold, red, blue. Op 6 bgrd.

Row 18. Cl 5 bgrd to where bgrd and blue in same hole. Drop bgrd. Cl blue, red, gold, red, blue, red. Add red. Op blue, red, gold, red, blue. St bgrd. Cl 5 bgrd.

Row 19. Op 5 bgrd. Cl blue, red, gold, red, blue, red. Add gold. Op red, blue, red, gold, red, blue. Drop st bgrd. Op 5 bgrd.

Row 20. Cl 4 bgrd to where bgrd and blue in same hole. Drop bgrd. Cl blue, red, gold, red, blue, red, gold. Add gold. Op red, blue, red, gold, red, blue. St bgrd. Cl 4 bgrd.

Row 21. Op 4 bgrd. Cl blue, rd, gold, red, glue, red, gold. Add blue. Op gold, red, blue, red, gold, red, blue. Drop st bgrd. Op 4 bgrd.

Row 22. Cl 3 bgrd to where bgrd and blue in same hole. Drop bgrd. Cl blue, red, gold, red, blue, red, gold, blue. Add blue. Op gold, red, blue, red, gold, red, blue. St bgrd. Cl 3 bgrd.

Row 23. Op 3 bgrd. Cl blue, red, gold, red, blue, red, gold, blue. Add red. Op blue, gold, red, blue, red, gold, red, blue. Drop st bgrd. Op 3 bgrd.

Row 24. Cl 2 bgrd to where bgrd and blue in same hole. Drop bgrd. Cl blue, red, gold, red, blue, red, gold, blue, red. Add red. Op blue, gold, red, blue, red, gold, red, blue. St bgrd. Cl 2 bgrd.

Row 25. Op 2 bgrd. Cl blue, red, gold. Add blue. St red. Cl blue, red, gold, blue, red Add blue. Op red, blue, gold, red, blue. St red. Add blue. Op gold, red, blue. Drop st bgrd. Op 2 bgrd.

Row 26. Cl 1 bgrd to where bgrd and blue in same hole. Drop bgrd. Cl blue, red, gold, blue. Drop st red. Cl blue, red, gold, blue, red, blue. Add blue. Op red, blue, gold, red, blue. Drop st red. Op blue, gold, red, blue. St bgrd. Cl 1 bgrd.

Row 27. Op 1 bgrd. Cl blue, red, gold, blue. Add bgrd. Op blue, red, gold, blue. St red. Cl blue. Add bgrd. Op blue. St red. Cl blue, gold, red, blue. Add bgrd. Op blue, gold, red, blue. Drop st bgrd. Op 1 bgrd.

Row 28. Bgrd and blue in same hole. Drop bgrd. Cl blue, red, gold, blue. Cl 1 bgrd. Add bgrd. Op blue, red, gold. St blue. Drop st red. Cl blue. Cl 1 bgrd. Add bgrd. Op blue. Drop st red. St blue. Cl gold, red, blue. Cl 1 bgrd. Add bgrd. Op blue, gold, red, blue. St bgrd.

Row 29. Add bgrd. Op blue. St red. Cl gold, blue. Add bgrd. Op 2 bgrd. Op blue, red. St gold. Drop st blue. Cl blue. Add bgrd. Op 2 bgrd. Op blue. Drop st blue. St gold. Cl red, blue. Add bgrd. Op 2 bgrd. Op blue, gold. St red. Cl blue. Drop st bgrd. Add bgrd.

Row 30. Cl 1 bgrd. Op blue. Drop st red. St gold. Cl blue. Cl 3 bgrd. Add bgrd. Op blue. St red. Drop st gold. Cl blue. Cl 3 bgrd. Add bgrd. Op blue. Drop st gold. St red. Cl blue. Cl 3 bgrd. Add bgrd. Op blue. St gold. Drop st red. Cl blue. Cl 1 bgrd.

Row 31. Op 1 bgrd. Add bgrd. Op blue. Drop st gold. St blue. Add bgrd. Op 4 bgrd. Op blue. Drop st red. St blue. Add bgrd. Op 4 bgrd. Op blue. Drop st red. St blue. Add bgrd. Op 4 bgrd. Op blue. Drop st gold. St blue. Add bgrd. Op 1 bgrd.

Row 32. 2 bgrd in same hole. Cl 1 bgrd; op 1 bgrd. St blue. Drop st blue. Cl 5 bgrd. Add bgrd. St blue. Drop st blue. Cl 5 bgrd. Add bgrd. St blue. Drop st blue. Cl 5 bgrd. Add bgrd. St blue. Drop st blue. Cl 2 bgrd.

Row 33. Op 2 bgrd. Drop st blue. Op 6 bgrd. Drop st blue. Op 6 bgrd. Drop st blue. Op 6 bgrd. Drop st blue. Op 2 bgrd.

Pattern #110

Row	
1	op
2	cl — R . . . 5 . R . . . 5 . R . . . 5 . R
3	op — . R R . . . 4 . R R . . . 4 . R R . . . 4 . R R .
4	cl — R B R . x3 . R B R . x3 . R B R . x3 . R B R
5	op — R G G R x2 R B B R x2 R B B R x2 R B G R
6	cl — R G B R x R B G B R x R B G B R x R B G R
7	op — R G G B R R B G G B R R B G G B R R B G B R
8	cl — R B G B R B G B G B R B G B G B R B G B R
9	op — R R B G B B G B B G B B G B B G B R R
10	cl — R R B G B G B R B G B G B R B G B G B R R
11	op — R G R B G G B R R B G G B R R B G G B R B R
12	cl — R B R B G B R G R B G B R G R B G B R B R
13	op — R R B R B B R G G R B B R G G R B B R B R R
14	cl — R R B R B R G B G R B R G B G R B R B R R
15	op — R G R B R R G B B G R R G B B G R R B R G R
16	cl — R G R B R G B R B G R G B R B G R B R G R
17	op — R G G R G G B R R B G G B R R B G B R G G R
18	cl — R G R B R G B R B G R G B R B G R B R G R
19	op — R G R B R R G B B G R R G B B G R R B R G R
20	cl — R R B R B R G B G R B R G B G R B R B R R
21	op — R R B R B B R G G R B B R G G R B B R B R R
22	cl — R B R B G B R G R B G B R G R B G B R B R
23	op — R B R B G G B R R B G G B R R B G G B R B R
24	cl — R R B G B G B R B G B G B R B G B G B R R
25	op — R R B G B B G B B G B B G B B G B R R
26	cl — R B G B R B G B G B R B G B G B R B G B R
27	op — R G G B R R B G G B R R B G G B R R B G B R
28	cl — R G B R x R B G B R x R B G B R x R B G R
29	op — R G G R x2 R B B R x2 R B B R x2 R B G R
30	cl — R B R . x3 . R B R . x3 . R B R . x3 . R B R
31	op — . R R . . . 4 . R R . . . 4 . R R . . . 4 . R R .
32	cl — R . . . 5 . R . . . 5 . R . . . 5 . R
33	op

R = Red
B = Blue
G = Gold

Directions for Pattern #110

This pattern shows how to make a *straight* line with hitched pulls. Look at the very edge red pulls on both sides of the pattern. To make it easier to see, draw this pattern out on your graph paper. Use a pencil to connect the red lines on the edge from Row 5 through Row 29.

Note: Add bgrd in these directions means to add one background pull. *Drop bgrd* in directions means to drop one background pull. *St bgrd* means to stand one background pull.

Row 1. Op 2 bgrd Add red. Op 6 bgrd. Add red. Op 6 bgrd. Add red. Op 6 bgrd. Add red. Op 2 bgrd.

Row 2. Cl 1 bgrd to where bgrd and red in same hole. Drop bgrd. Cl red. Add red. St bgrd. Cl 4 bgrd to where bgrd and red in same hole. Drop bgrd. Cl red. Add red. St bgrd. Cl 4 bgrd to where bgrd and red in same hole. Drop bgrd. Cl red. Add red. St bgrd. Cl 4 bgrd to where bgrd and red in same hole. Drop bgrd. Cl red. Add red. St bgrd. Cl bgrd.

Row 3. Op 1 bgrd. Cl red. Add blue. Op red. Drop st bgrd. Op 4 bgrd. Cl red. Add blue. Op red. Drop st bgrd. Op 4 bgrd. Cl red. Add blue. Op red. Drop st bgrd. Op 4 bgrd. Cl red. Add blue. Op red. Drop st bgrd. Op 1 bgrd.

Row 4. Bgrd and red in same hole. Drop bgrd. Cl red. Add gold. Op blue, red. St bgrd. Cl 2 bgrd to where bgrd and red in same hole. Drop bgrd. Cl red, blue. Add blue. Op red. St bgrd. Cl 2 bgrd to where bgrd and red in same hole. Drop bgrd. Cl red, blue. Add blue. Op red. St bgrd. Cl 2 bgrd to where bgrd and red in same hole. Drop bgrd. Cl red, blue. Add gold. Op red. St bgrd.

Row 5. Op red, gold, blue, red. Drop st bgrd. Op 2 bgrd. Cl red, blue. Add gold. Op blue, red. Drop st bgrd. Op 2 bgrd. Cl red, blue. Add gold. Op blue, red. Drop st bgd. Op 2 bgrd. Cl red, blue, gold, red. Drop st bgrd.

Row 6. Cl red. Add blue. Op gold, blue, red. St bgrd. Bgrd and red in same hole. Drop bgrd. Cl red, blue, gold. Add gold. Op blue, red. St bgrd. Bgrd and red in same hole. Drop bgrd. Cl red, blue, gold. Add gold. Op blue, red. St bgrd. Bgrd and red in same hole. Drop bgrd. Cl red, blue, gold. Add blue. Op red.

Row 7. Op red, blue, gold, blue, red. Drop st bgrd. St red. Cl blue, gold. Add blue. Op gold, blue, red. Drop st bgrd. St red. Cl blue, gold. Add blue. Op gold, blue, red. Drop st bgrd. St red. Cl blue, gold, blue, red.

Row 8. Cl red. Add red. Op blue, gold, blue. St red. Drop st red. Cl blue, gold, blue. Add blue. Op gold, blue. St red. Drop st red. Cl blue, gold, blue. Add blue. Op gold, blue. St red. Drop st red. Cl blue, gold, blue. Add red. Op red.

Row 9. Op red, red, blue, gold, blue. Drop st red. St blue. Cl gold, blue. Add red. Op blue, gold, blue. Drop st red. St blue. Cl gold, blue. Add red. Op blue, gold, blue. Drop st red. St blue. Cl gold, blue, red, red.

Row 10. Cl red. Add blue. Op red, blue, gold. St blue. Drop st blue. Cl gold, blue, red. Add red. Op blue, gold. St blue. Drop st blue. Cl gold, blue, red. Add red. Op blue, gold. St blue. Drop st blue. Cl gold, blue, red. Add blue. Op red.

Row 11. Op red, blue, red, blue, gold. Drop st blue. St gold. Cl blue, red. Add gold. Op red, blue, gold. Drop st blue. St gold. Cl blue, red. Add gold. Op red, blue, gold. Drop st blue. St gold. Cl blue, red, blue, red.

Row 12. Cl red. Add red. Op blue, red, blue. St gold. Drop st gold. Cl blue, red, gold. Add gold. Op red, blue. St gold. Drop st gold. Cl blue, red, gold. Add gold. Op red, blue. St gold. Drop st gold. Cl blue, red, blue. Add red. Op red.

Row 13. Op red, red, blue, red, blue. Drop st gold. St blue. Cl red, gold. Add blue. Op gold, red, blue. Drop st gold. St blue. Cl red, gold. Add blue. Op gold, red, blue. Drop st gold. St blue. Cl red, blue, red, red.

Note: The gold pulls added in Row 14 and Row 16 have a unique way of being hitched. These gold pulls will be dropped in Row 18 and Row 20. Draw connecting pencil lines on your graph paper to see how these pulls are hitched.

Row 14. Cl red. Add gold. Op red, blue, red. St blue. Drop st blue. Cl red, gold, blue. Add blue. Op gold, red. St blue. Drop st blue. Cl red, gold, blue. Add blue. Op gold, red. St blue. Drop st blue. Cl red, blue, red. Add gold. Op red.

Row 15. Op red, gold, red, blue, red. Drop st blue. St red. Cl gold, blue. Add red. Op blue, gold, red. Drop st blue. St red. Cl gold, blue. Add red. Op blue, gold, red. Drop st blue. St red. Cl blue, red, gold, red.

Row 16. Cl red. Add gold. Op gold, red, blue. St red. Drop st red. Cl gold, blue, red. Add red. Op blue, gold. St red. Drop st red. Cl gold, blue, red. Add red. Op blue, gold. St red. Drop st red. Cl blue, red, gold. Add gold. Op red.

Row 17. Op red, gold. St gold. Cl red, blue. Drop st red. Add red. Op gold, blue. St red. Cl red, blue, gold. Drop st red. Add red. Op gold, blue. St red. Cl red, blue, gold. Drop st red. Add red. Op blue, red. St gold. Cl gold, red.

Row 18. Cl red, gold. Drop st gold. Cl red, blue, red. Add red. Op gold, blue. Drop st red. St red. Cl blue, gold, red. Add red. Op gold, blue. Drop st red. St red. Cl blue, gold, red. Add red. Op blue, red. Drop st gold. Op gold, red.

Row 19. Op red. St gold. Cl red, blue, red. Add blue. Op red, gold, blue. Drop st red. St blue. Cl gold, red. Add blue. Op red, gold, blue. Drop st red. St blue. Cl gold, red. Add blue. Op red, blue, red. St gold. Cl red.

Row 20. Cl red. Drop st gold. Cl red, blue, red, blue. Add blue. Op red, gold. St blue. Drop st blue. Cl gold, red, blue. Add blue. Op red, gold. St blue. Drop st blue. Cl gold, red, blue. Add blue. Op red, blue, red. Drop st gold. Op red.

Row 21. Op red. St red. Cl blue, red, blue. Add gold. Op blue, red, gold. Drop st blue. St gold. Cl red, blue. Add gold. Op blue, red, gold. Drop st blue. St gold. Cl red, blue. Add gold. Op blue, red, blue. St red. Cl red.

Row 22. Cl red. Drop st red. Cl blue, red, blue, gold. Add gold. Op blue, red. St gold. Drop st gold. Cl red, blue, gold. Add gold. Op blue, red. St gold. Drop st gold. Cl red, blue, gold. Add gold. Op blue, red, blue. Drop st red. Op red.

Row 23. Op red. St blue. Cl red, blue, gold. Add blue. Op gold, blue, red. Drop st gold. St red. Cl blue, gold. Add blue. Op gold, blue, red. Drop st gold. St red. Cl blue, gold. Add blue. Op gold, blue, red. St blue. Cl red.

Row 24. Cl red. Drop st blue. Cl red, blue, gold, blue. Add blue. Op gold, blue. St red. Drop st red. Cl blue, gold, blue. Add blue. Op gold, blue. St red. Drop st red. Cl blue, gold, blue. Add blue. Op gold, blue, red. Drop st blue. Op red.

Row 25. Op red. St red. Cl blue, gold, blue. Add red. Op blue, gold, blue. Drop st red. St blue. Cl gold, blue. Add red. Op blue, gold, blue. Drop st red. St blue. Cl gold, blue. Add red. Op blue, gold, blue. St red. Cl red.

Row 26. Cl red. Drop st red. Cl blue, gold, blue, red. Add red. Op blue, gold. St blue. Drop st blue. Cl gold, blue, red. Add red. Op blue, gold. St blue. Drop st blue. Cl gold, blue, red. Add red. Op blue, gold, blue. Drop st red. Op red.

Row 27. Op red. St blue. Cl gold, blue, red. Add bgrd. Op red, blue, gold. Drop st blue. St gold. Cl blue, red. Add bgd. Op red, blue, gold. Drop st blue. St gold. Cl blue, red. Add bgd. Op red, blue, gold. St blue. Cl red.

Row 28. Cl red. Drop st blue. Cl gold, blue, red. Cl 1 bgrd. Add bgrd. Op red, blue. St gold. Drop st gold. Cl blue, red. Cl 1 bgrd. Add bgrd. Op red, blue. St gold. Drop st gold. Cl blue, red. Cl 1 bgrd. Add bgrd. Op red, blue, gold. Drop st blue. Op red.

Row 29. Add bgd. Op red. St gold. Cl blue, red. Add bgrd. Op 2 bgrd. Op red, blue. Drop st gold. St blue. Cl red. Add bgrd. Op 2 bgrd. Op red, blue. Drop st gold. St blue. Cl red. Add bgrd. Op 2 bgrd. Op red, blue. St gold. Cl red. Add bgrd.

Row 30. Cl 1 bgrd. Op red. Drop st gold. St blue. Cl red. Cl 3 bgrd. Add bgrd. Op red. St blue. Drop st blue. Cl red. Cl 3 bgrd. Add bgrd. Op red. St blue. Drop st blue Cl red. Cl 3 bgd. Add bgrd. Op rd. St blue. Drop st gold. Cl red. Cl 1 bgrd.

Row 31. Op 1 bgrd. Add bgrd. Op red. Drop st blue. St red. Add bgrd. Op 4 bgrd. Op red. Drop st blue. St red. Add bgrd. Op 4 bgd. Op red. Drop st blue. St red. Add bgrd. Op 4 bgrd. Op red. Drop st blue. St red. Add bgrd. Op 1 bgrd.

Row 32. 2 bgrd in same hole. Cl 1 bgrd; op 1 bgrd. St red. Drop st red. Cl 5 bgrd. Add bgrd. St red. Drop st red. Cl 5 bgrd. Add bgrd. St red. Drop st red. Cl 5 bgd. Add bgrd. St red. Drop st red. Cl 2 bgrd.

Row 33. Op 2 bgrd. Drop st red. Op 6 bgrd. Drop st red. Op 6 bgrd. Drop st red. Op 6 bgrd. Drop st red. Op 2 bgrd.

Chapter 21

In the Round Patterns

All hitching is done *in the round*, a circular motion in which each row meets the next row. This chapter focuses on *in the round* patterns. These are patterns which go all the way around the hitched item. This is not the same thing as the spiral patterns that are closed hitches only. This chapter has 2 traditional *in the round* patterns with directions.

General Information

In the round patterns are used mainly on reins, key fobs, bracelets, and headstalls which are not pressed. Rope is the core material for reins and headstalls. Bendable metal is the core for bracelets. Historically, walking canes were hitched with *in the round* patterns.

Graphing In the Round Patterns

Graphing *in the round* patterns is more difficult than patterns for pressed items with cross hitch borders. The mind has to imagine the pattern meeting itself in each row.

The closed hitch rows are unusual in graphing these patterns. To make the graphing work, pulls are placed outside of the perimeters of the graphed pattern. Broken lines are used to show this. These broken lines can be on either side of the pattern depending on the pattern. See graphed pattern #202 with broken lines on the left side.

Three things can help in understanding this better:

1. See Pattern #201. There is a triangle around some broken lines on the pattern. This is the right side of the diamond. The actual graphed part is the solid lines on rows 11 through 23. On some patterns the lines can be extended out in order to understand what needs to be hitched next.
2. Make an actual tube with your graph paper. Have each row meet itself. Visually see what is going on. To do this transfer a pattern in this chapter to graph paper. Cut the graph paper so each row can meet itself. Tape it together this way if it helps to understand.
3. Hitch the patterns. As always, the best way to understand is hands on experience.

Pattern #201

Row	
1	* * *5* * / * * * * * *10* * * * / * * *5* *
2	R * * * * 9 * * * R
3	* * * R R * * * * *8* * R R * * *4*
4	R G R * * * *7* * R G R
5	* *3* R G G R * * *6* R G G R * *3*
6	R G B G R * * *5* R G B G R
7	*2* R G B B G R * * *4* R G B B G R *2*
8	R G B R B G R * *3* R G B R B G R
9	* R G B R R B G R */* R G B R R B G R *
10	* R G B R B G R * G * R G B R B G R * G
11	G * R G B B G R * G G * R G B B G R * G
12	G * R G B G R * G R G * R G B G R * G R
13	R G * R G G R * G R R G * R G G R * G R
14	R G * R G R * G R B R G * R G R * G R B
15	B R G * R R * G R B B R G * R R * G R B
16	B R G * R * G R B G B R G * R * G R B G
17	G B R G */* G R B G G B R G */* G R B G
18	B R G * R * G R B G B R G * R * G R B G
19	B R G * R R * G R B B R G * R R * G R B
20	R G * R G R * G R B R G * R G R * G R B
21	R G * R G G R * G R R G * R G G R * G R
22	G * R G B G R * G R G * R G B G R * G R
23	G * R G B B G R * G G * R G B B G R * G
24	* R G B R B G R * G * R G B R B G R * G
25	* R G B R R B G R */* R G B R R B G R *
26	* R G B R B G R * *3* R G B R B G R
27	* R G B B G R * * *4* R G B B G R *2*
28	* R G B G R * * *5* * R G B G R
29	* R G G R * * * *6* * R G G R * *3*
30	* R G R * * * * *7* * R G R
31	* R R * * * * *8* * R R * * *4*
32	* R * * * *9* * * * R
33	* * *5* */* * * * *10* * * */* * *5* *

R = Red
B = Black
G = Gold

Directions for Pattern #201

Row 1. Op 5 bgrd. Add red. Op 10 bgrd. Add red. Op 5 bgrd.

Row 2. Cl 4 bgrd to where bgrd and red in same hole. Drop bgrd. Cl red. Add red. St bgrd. Cl 8 bgrd to where bgrd and red in same hole. Drop bgrd. Cl red. Add red. St bgrd. Cl 4 bgrd.

Row 3. Op 4 bgrd. Cl red. Add gold. Op red. Drop st bgrd. Op 8 bgrd. Cl red. Add gold. Op red. Drop st bgrd. Op 4 bgrd.

Row 4. Cl 3 bgrd to where bgrd and red in same hole. Drop bgrd. Cl red, gold. Add gold. Op red. St bgrd. Cl 6 bgrd to where bgrd and red in same hole. Cl red, gold. Add gold. Op red. St bgrd. Cl 3 bgrd.

Row 5. Op 3 bgrd. Cl red, gold. Add black. Op gold, red. Drop st bgrd. Op 6 bgrd. Cl red, gold. Add black. Op gold, red. Drop st bgrd. Op 3 bgrd.

Row 6. Cl 2 bgrd to where bgrd and red in same hole. Drop bgrd. Cl red, gold, black. Add black. Op gold, red. St bgrd. Cl 4 bgrd to where bgrd and red in same hole. Cl red, gold, black. Add black. Op gold, red. St bgrd. Cl 2 bgrd.

Row 7. Op 2 bgrd. Cl red, gold, black. Add red. Op black, gold, red. Drop st bgrd. Op 4 bgrd. Cl red, gold, black. Add red. Op black, gold, red. Drop st bgrd. Op 2 bgrd.

Row 8. Cl 1 bgrd to where bgrd and red in same hole. Drop bgrd. Cl red, gold, black, red. Add red. Op black, gold, red. St bgrd. Cl 2 bgrd to where bgrd and red in same hole. Drop bgrd. Cl red, gold, black, red. Add red. Op black, gold, red. St bgrd. Cl 1 bgrd.

Row 9. Op 1 bgrd. Op red, gold, black. St red. Cl red, black, gold, red. Drop st bgrd. Cl 1 bgrd. Add gold. Op 1 bgrd. Op red, gold, black. St red. Cl red, black, gold, red. Cl 1 bgrd. Add gold.

Row 10. Op bgrd, red, gold, black. Drop st red. St red. Cl black, gold, red, bgrd, gold. Add gold. Op bgrd, red, gold, black. Drop st red. St red. Cl black, gold, red, bgrd, gold. Add gold.

Row 11. Op bgrd, red, gold, black. Drop st red. St black. Cl gold, red, bgrd, gold. Add red. Op gold, bgrd, red, gold, black. Drop st red. St black. Cl gold, red, bgrd, gold. Add red. Op gold.

Row 12. Op bgrd, red, gold. St black. Drop st black. Cl gold, red, bgrd, gold, red. Add red. Op gold, bgrd, red, gold. St black. Drop st black. Cl gold, red, bgrd, gold, red. Add red. Op gold.

Row 13. Op bgrd, red, gold. Drop st black. St gold. Cl red, bgrd, gold, red. Add black. Op red, gold, bgrd, red, gold. Drop st black. St gold. Cl red, bgrd, gold, red. Add black. Op red, gold.

Row 14. Op bgrd, red. St gold. Drop st gold. Cl red, bgrd, gold, red, black. Add black. Op red, gold, bgrd, red. St gold. Drop st gold. Cl red, bgrd, gold, red, black. Add black. Op red, gold.

Row 15. Op bgrd, red. Drop st gold. St red. Cl bgrd, gold, red, black. Add gold. Op black, red, gold, bgrd, red. Drop st gold. St red. Cl bgrd, gold, red, black. Add gold. Op black, red, gold.

Row 16. Op bgrd. St red. Drop st red. Cl bgrd, gold, red, black, gold. Add gold. Op black, red, gold, bgrd. St red. Drop st red. Cl bgrd, gold, red, black, gold. Add gold. Op black, red, gold.

Row 17. Cl bgrd. Drop st red. Add red. Op bgrd, gold, red, black. St gold. Cl gold, black, red, gold, bgrd. Drop st red. Add red. Op bgrd, gold, red, black. St gold. Cl gold, black, red, gold.

Row 18. Cl bgrd. Cl red. Add red. Op bgrd, gold, red, black. Drop st gold. St gold. Cl black, red, gold, bgrd, red. Add red. Op bgrd, gold, red, black. Drop st gold. St gold. Cl black, red, gold.

Row 19. Cl bgrd, red. Add gold. Op red, bgrd, gold, red, black. Drop st gold. St black. Cl red, gold, bgrd, red. Add gold. Op red, bgrd, gold, red, black. Drop st gold. St black. Cl red, gold.

Row 20. Cl bgrd, red, gold. Add gold. Op red, bgrd, gold, red. St black. Drop st black. Cl red, gold, bgrd, red, gold. Add gold. Op red, bgrd, gold, red. St black. Drop st black. Cl red, gold.

Row 21. Cl bgrd, red, gold. Add black. Op gold, red, bgrd, gold, red. Drop st black. St red. Cl gold, bgrd, red, gold. Add black. Op gold, red, bgrd, gold, red. Drop st black. St red. Cl gold.

Row 22. Cl bgrd, red, gold, black. Add black. Op gold, red, bgrd, gold. St red. Drop st red. Cl gold, bgrd, red, gold, black. Add black. Op gold, red, bgrd, gold. St red. Drop st red. Cl gold.

Row 23. Cl bgrd, red, gold, black. Add red. Op black, gold, red, bgrd, gold. Drop st red. St gold. Cl bgrd, red, gold, black. Add red. Op black, gold, red, bgrd, gold. Drop st red. St gold.

Row 24. Cl bgrd, red, gold, black, red. Add red. Op black, gold, red, bgrd. St gold. Drop st gold. Cl bgrd, red, gold, black, red. Add red. Op black gold, red, bgrd. St gold. Drop st gold.

Row 25. Op bgrd, red, gold, black. St red. Cl red, black, gold, red. Add bgrd. Op bgrd. Drop st gold. Op bgrd, red, gold, black. St red. Cl red, black, gold, red. Add bgrd. Op bgrd. Drop st gold.

Row 26. Put masking tape on the next bgrd pull. This will now be the start point pull. Cl start point bgrd pull. Add bgrd. Op red, gold, black. Drop st red. St red. Cl black, gold, red. Cl 3 bgrd. Add bgrd. Op red, gold, black. Drop st red. St red. Cl black, gold, red. Cl 2 bgrd.

Row 27. Op 2 bgrd. Op red, gold, black. Drop st red. St black. Cl gold, red. Add bgrd. Op 4 bgrd. Op red, gold, black. Drop st red. St black. Cl gold, red. Add bgrd. Op 2 bgrd.

Row 28. Cl 2 bgrd. Add bgrd. Op red, gold. St black. Drop st black. Cl gold, red. Cl 5 bgrd. Add bgrd. Op red, gold. St black. Drop st black. Cl gold, red. Cl 3 bgrd.

Row 29. Op 3 bgrd. Op red, gold. Drop st black. St gold. Cl red. Add bgrd. Op 6 bgrd. Op red, gold. Drop st black. St gold.. Cl red. Add bgrd. Op 3 bgrd.

Row 30. Cl 3 bgrd. Add bgrd. Op red. St gold. Drop st gold. Cl red. Cl 7 bgrd. Add bgrd. Op red. St gold. Drop st gold. Cl red. Cl 4 bgrd.

Row 31. Op 4 bgrd. Op red. Drop st gold. St red. Add bgrd. Op 8 bgrd. Op red. Drop st gold. St red. Add bgrd. Op 4 bgrd.

Row 32. Cl 4 bgrd. Add bgrd. St red. Drop st red. Cl 9 bgrd. Add bgrd. St red. Drop st red. Cl 5 bgrd.

Row 33. Op 5 bgrd. Drop st red. Op 10 bgrd. Drop st red. Op 5 bgrd.

Pattern #202

x²	x	/	x	α	x	x⁵	/	x	α	x	x⁵	/	x	α	x⁵	x	/	x	x³	x	1 op
	R	α	x	⁴x	x	R	α	α	α⁴	α	R	α	α	α⁴	α	R			x²	x	2 cl
	R	R	α	x³	R	R	α	α³	x	R	R	α	α³	x	R	R	x²	x			3 op
R	B	R	x	²x	R	B	R	α²	x	R	B	R	x	²x	R	B	R				4 cl
R	B	B	R	x	R	B	B	R	x	R	B	B	R	x	R	B	B	R	x		5 op
B	G	B	R	R	B	G	B	R	R	B	G	B	R	R	B	G	B	R			6 cl
B	G	G	B	R	B	G	G	B	R	B	G	G	B	R	B	G	G	B	R		7 op
G	R	G	B	B	G	R	G	B	B	G	R	G	B	B	G	R	G	B			8 cl
G	R	R	G	B	G	R	R	G	B	G	R	R	G	B	G	R	R	G	B		9 op
R	B	R	G	G	R	B	R	G	G	R	B	R	G	G	R	B	R	G			10 cl
R	B	B	R	G	R	B	B	R	G	R	B	B	R	G	R	B	B	R	G		11 op
B	G	B	R	R	B	G	B	R	R	B	G	B	R	R	B	G	B	R			12 cl
B	G	G	B	R	B	G	G	B	R	B	G	G	B	R	B	G	G	B	R		13 op
B	G	B	R	R	B	G	B	R	R	B	G	B	R	R	B	G	B	R			14 cl
R	B	R	G	G	R	B	R	G	G	R	B	R	G	G	R	B	R	G	G		15 op
R	B	R	G	G	R	B	R	G	G	R	B	R	G	G	R	B	R	G			16 cl
G	R	R	G	B	G	R	R	G	B	G	R	R	G	B	G	R	R	G	B		17 op
G	R	G	B	B	G	R	G	B	B	G	R	G	B	B	G	R	G	B			18 cl
B	G	G	B	R	B	G	G	B	R	B	G	G	B	R	B	G	G	B	R		19 op
B	G	B	R	R	B	G	B	R	R	B	G	B	R	R	B	G	B	R			20 cl
R	B	B	R	x	R	B	B	R	x	R	B	B	R	x	R	B	B	R	x		21 op
R	B	R	x	²x	R	B	R	α²	x	R	B	R	α²	x	R	B	R				22 cl
	R	R	α	α³	x	R	R	α	α³	R	R	α	α³	x	R	R	x²	x			23 op
	R	α	α	α⁴	α	R	α	α	α⁴	x	R	x	α	⁴x	α	R					24 cl
x²	x	/	x	α	x	x⁵	/	x	α	x	α⁵	/	x	α	x⁵	α	/	x	α³	x	25 op

R = Red
B = Blue
G = Gold

Directions for Pattern #202

Row 1. Op 2 bgrd. Add red. Op 5 bgrd. Add red. Op 5 bgrd. Add red. Op 5 bgrd. Add red. Op 3 bgrd.

Row 2. Cl 1 bgrd to where bgrd and red in same hole. Drop bgrd. Cl red. Add red. St bgrd. Cl 3 bgrd to where bgrd and red in same hole. Drop bgrd. Cl red. Add red. St bgrd. Cl 3 bgrd to where bgrd and red in same hole. Drop bgrd. Cl red. Add red. St bgrd. Cl 3 bgrd to where bgrd and red in same hole. Drop bgrd. Cl red. Add red. St bgrd. Cl 2 bgrd.

Row 3. Op 1 bgrd. Cl red. Add blue. Op red. Drop st bgrd. Op 3 bgrd. Cl red. Add blue. Op red. Drop st bgrd. Op 3 bgrd. Cl red. Add blue. Op red. Drop st bgrd. Op 3 bgrd. Cl red. Add blue. Op red. Drop st bgrd. Op 2 bgrd.

Row 4. Bgrd and red in same hole. Drop bgrd. Cl red, blue. Add blue. Op red. St bgrd. Cl 1 bgrd to where bgrd and red in same hole. Drop bgrd. Cl red, blue. Add blue. Op red. St bgrd. Cl 1 bgrd to where bgrd and red in same hole. Drop bgrd. Cl red, blue. Add blue. Op red. St bgrd. Cl 1 bgrd to where bgrd and red in same hole. Cl red, blue. Add blue. Op red. St bgrd. Cl 1 bgrd.

Row 5. Cl red, blue. Add gold. Op blue, red. Drop st bgrd. St bgrd. Cl red, blue. Add gold. Op blue, red. Drop st bgrd. St bgrd. Cl red, blue. Add gold. Op blue, red. Drop st bgrd. St bgrd. Cl red, blue. Add gold. Op blue, red. Drop st bgrd. St bgrd.

Row 6. St red. Cl blue, gold. Add gold. Op blue, red. Drop st bgrd. St red. Cl blue, gold. Add gold. Op blue, red. Drop st bgrd. St red. Cl blue, gold. Add gold. Op blue, red. Drop st bgrd. St red. Cl blue, gold. Add gold. Op blue, red. Drop st bgrd.

Row 7. Drop st red. Cl blue, gold. Add red. Op gold, blue. St red. Drop st red. Cl blue, gold. Add red. Op gold, blue. St red. Drop st red. Cl blue, gold. Add red. Op gold, blue. St red. Drop st red. Cl blue, gold. Add red. Op gold, blue. St red.

Row 8. St blue. Cl gold, red. Add red. Op gold, blue. Drop st red. St blue. Cl gold, red. Add red. Op gold, blue. Drop st red. St blue. Cl gold, red. Add red. Op gold, blue. Drop st red. St blue. Cl gold, red. Add red. Op gold, blue. Drop st red.

Row 9. Drop st blue. Cl gold, red. Add blue. Op red, gold. St blue. Drop st blue. Cl gold, red. Add blue. Op red, gold. St blue. Drop st blue. Cl gold, red. Add blue. Op red, gold. St blue. Drop st blue. Cl gold, red. Add blue. Op red, gold. St blue.

Row 10. St gold. Cl red, blue. Add blue. Op red, gold. Drop st blue. St gold. Cl red, blue. Add blue. Op red, gold. Drop st blue. St gold. Cl red, blue. Add blue. Op red, gold. Drop st blue. St gold. Cl red, blue. Add blue. Op red, gold. Drop st blue.

Row 11. Drop st gold. Cl red, blue. Add gold. Op blue, red. St gold. Drop st gold. Cl red, blue. Add gold. Op blue, red. St gold. Drop st gold. Cl red, blue. Add gold. Op blue, red. St gold. Drop st gold. Cl red, blue. Add gold. Op blue, red. St gold.

Row 12. St red. Cl blue, gold. Add gold. Op blue, red. Drop st gold. St red. Cl blue, gold. Add gold. Op blue, red. Drop st gold. St red. Cl blue, gold. Add gold. Op blue, red. Drop st gold. St red. Cl blue, gold. Add gold. Op blue, red. Drop st gold.

Row 13. Drop st red. Add red. Op blue. St gold. Cl gold, blue, red. Drop st red. Add red. Op blue. St gold. Cl gold, blue, red. Drop st red. Add red. Op blue. St gold. Cl gold, blue, red. Drop st red. Add red. Op blue. St gold. Cl gold, blue, red.

Row 14. Op red, blue. Drop st gold. St gold. Cl blue, red. Add gold. Op red, blue. Drop st gold. St gold. Cl blue, red. Add gold. Op red, blue. Drop st gold. St gold. Cl blue, red. Add gold. Op red, blue. Drop st gold. St gold. Cl blue, red. Add gold.

Row 15. Add gold. Op red, blue. Drop st gold. St blue. Cl red, gold. Add gold. Op red, blue. Drop st gold. St blue. Cl red, gold. Add gold. Op red, blue. Drop st gold. St blue. Cl red, gold. Add gold. Op red, blue. Drop st gold. St blue. Cl red, gold.

Row 16. Op gold, red. St blue. Drop st blue. Cl red, gold. Add blue. Op gold, red. St blue. Drop st blue. Cl red, gold. Add blue. Op gold, red. St blue. Drop st blue. Cl red, gold. Add blue. Op gold, red. St blue. Drop st blue. Cl red, gold. Add blue.

Row 17. Add blue. Op gold, red. Drop st blue. St red. Cl gold, blue. Add blue. Op gold, red. Drop st blue. St red. Cl gold, blue. Add blue. Op gold, red. Drop st blue. St red. Cl gold, blue. Add blue. Op gold, red. Drop st blue. St red. Cl gold, blue.

Row 18. Op blue, gold. St red. Drop st red. Cl gold, blue. Add red. Op blue, gold. St red. Drop st red. Cl gold, blue. Add red. Op blue, gold. St red. Drop st red. Cl gold, blue. Add red. Op blue, gold. St red. Drop st red. Cl gold, blue. Add red.

Row 19. Add red. Op blue, gold. Drop st red. St gold. Cl blue, red. Add red. Op blue, gold. Drop st red. St gold. Cl blue, red. Add red. Op blue, gold. Drop st red. St gold. Cl blue, red. Add red. Op blue, gold. Drop st red. St gold. Cl blue, red.

Row 20. Op red, blue. St gold. Drop st gold. Cl blue, red. Add bgrd. Op red, blue. St gold. Drop st gold. Cl blue, red. Add bgrd. Op red, blue. St gold. Drop st gold. Cl blue, red. Add bgrd. Op red, blue. St gold. Drop st gold. Cl blue, red. Add bgrd.

Row 21. Op red, blue. Drop st gold. St blue. Cl red. Add bgrd. Op bgrd, red, blue. Drop gold. St blue. Cl red. Add bgrd. Op bgrd, red, blue. Drop st gold. St blue. Cl red. Add bgrd. Op bgrd, red, blue. Drop st gold. St blue. Cl red. Add bgrd. Op bgrd.

Row 22. Add bgrd. Mark this bgrd with masking tape. This will be the start point pull. Op red. St blue. Drop st blue. Cl red. Cl 2 bgrd. Add bgrd. Op red. St blue. Drop st blue. Cl red. Cl 2 bgrd. Add bgrd. Op red. St blue. Drop st blue. Cl red. Cl 2 bgrd. Add bgrd. Op red. St blue. Drop st blue. Cl red. Cl 2 bgrd.

Row 23. Op bgrd. Op red. Drop st blue. St red. Add bgrd. Op 3 bgrd. Op red. Drop st blue. St red. Add bgrd. Op 3 bgrd. Op red. Drop st blue. St red. Add bgrd. Op 3 bgrd. Op red. Drop st blue. St red. Add bgrd. Op 2 bgrd.

Row 24. Cl bgrd. Add bgrd. St red. Drop st red. Cl 4 bgrd. Add bgrd. St red. Drop st red. Cl 4 bgrd. Add bgrd. St red. Drop st red. Cl 4 bgrd. Add bgrd. St red. Drop st red. Cl 3 bgrd.

Row 25. Op 2 bgrd. Drop st red. Op 5 bgrd. Drop st red. Op 5 bgrd. Drop st red. Op 5 bgrd. Drop st red. Op 3 bgrd.

Notes

About the Author

Certain facts can never be swayed. So it is true with *once a Montanan, always a Montanan*. My 5th generation roots are in Montana wherever I may otherwise land. My husband, Ron, and I moved to Washington state in 1992. After sticking it out with city living for 1 ½ years, we moved to Kettle Falls, the nearest place that looked like Montana. Here we've built our house, with the help of family and a few friends.

Hitching as a vocation came to me through the back door. I grew up on a farm in Montana and was working as a commercial beekeeper in the family business when I got laid off due to drought and farm economics.

Ron was Hobby Director at Montana State Prison. Hitched horsehair was just beginning a resurgence as a collectible and functional art form. We knew there was a demand for high quality hitched items. I became self-taught, taking over a year to learn. I could not learn from inmates as it was a conflict of interest with Ron's job.

Inspiration has played the major role for me learning how to hitch and write this book. Learning wasn't always easy. Some days I felt totally overwhelmed; some days I wanted to give up. Luckily there were more good days and a feeling of accomplishment at working at this art form

Ron was continually encouraging, with constructive criticism when necessary. I used him for my quality control. He believed I could learn hitching. So I believed I could too. Hitching catches hold of a person, to the point of dreaming and thinking about it continually.

I credit Ron with taking part in this hitched horsehair resurgence. Hitching is the oldest hobby in the Montana prison system, going back to the old territorial prison. When he started as Hobby Director, two men knew how to hitch. Ron recognized it as a valid art form, and took the necessary steps to build up both this hobby, and the entire program. Workshops were taught, there was an increase in custom orders, and people traveling through Deer Lodge, Montana, knew the Hobby Store sold hitched items.

When we started our business, Hitching Tails, we had 3 goals in mind:
- I would learn how to hitch.
- We would write the book.
- Workshops on how to hitch would develop.

Until the book was written, we did not want to teach hitching. We knew people needed information on how to hitch as there is so little available. We wanted to make it easier for people to learn, so they could learn in minutes what it may have taken me weeks or months to learn. This book is the natural outcome of that.

We are fortunate to have become acquainted with Sam and Ellie Henderson. Sam was a retired rancher when he came to us to learn how to hitch. Sam has managed ranches from the Conejo Ranch in Los Angeles to Charles Lindbergh's ranch in Montana, and points in between. It soon became apparent that Sam was the person to learn from the rough draft of the book and critique it for us from a beginner's viewpoint. A friendship developed with Sam and Ellie. We've learned more from them and their experiences all over the West than they've learned from us.

Ron and I believe we are the first to place hitched horsehair inlays in sterling silver, thus producing belt buckles, bolos, barrettes, necklaces, and pins. We liken these items to the old Southwest pawn, where each piece was handmade, without any cast silverwork. Hitched inlays are more difficult to inlay than stones. I provide the hitched inlays, and Ron does the silverwork.

He has also developed a sterling silver banding to cover the joint where the hitched blank and leather are sewn together. This looks simple, but is a complex process. The silver banding cannot slip on the belt, nor can it cut into the leather or hitching. Ron brings the expertise of running a business, with sales and marketing. He is an internationally known bowyer (master bowmaker, as in longbows and arrows).

We are moving into more pictorial designs, such as our Double Eagle, Eagle (both copyrighted), and End of the Trail.

My formal education includes a B.S. from Montana State University but I never was inclined to pursue what I had studied there. I find more satisfaction from the various work I've done, including beekeeping and hitching. It is no coincidence that these are related to a rural and western lifestyle. Both this and my diverse ethnic heritage shows in the art I do.

We participate in the following shows: I See By Your Outfit That You Are a Cowboy, Sun Valley Center for the Arts, Sun Valley, Idaho; Beyond the 98th Meridian: Images of the American West, Dry Creek Arts Fellowship, Sedona, Arizona; Cowboy Classics, Phoenix, Arizona; Trappings of the American West, Coconino Center for the Arts, Flagstaff, Arizona; Spokane Western Art Show, Spokane, Washington. We appreciate that there are organizations, staff, and volunteers who provide a venue for western art.

Appendix

Supplier—Finished Hitched Products & *Hitched Horsehair: The Complete Guide for Self-Learning*

>Shoni Maulding
>Hitching Tails
>P.O. Box 1123
>Kettle Falls, WA 99141
>509-738-6944

Suppliers of Horsehair, Leather, Findings, & *Hitched Horsehair: The Complete Guide for Self-Learning*

ALKINCO Hair Company
264 West 40th Street
New York, NY 10018
Tel: 212-719-3070
Tel: 1-800-HAIR-118
Fax: 212-764-7804

Berman Leathercraft
25 Melcher St.
Boston, MA 02210-1599

Hitching Post Supply
10312 210th St. S.E.
Snohomish, WA 98296
Tel: 360-668-2349
Tel: 1-800-689-9971
Fax: 425-487-1947

Indian Jewelers Supply
601 East Coal Ave.
Gallup, NM 87301-6005
Tel: 505-722-4451
Fax: 505-722-4172

Leather Factory
P.O. Box 50429
Fort Worth, TX 76105

Rings and Things
P.O. Box 450
Spokane, WA 99210-0450
Tel: 509-624-8565
Fax: 509-838-2602

Tandy Leather
P.O. Box 791
Fort Worth, TX 76101
or contact local Tandy stores

Wagman Primus Group, LP
10 Strawberry Street
Philadelphia, PA 19106
Tel: 215-923-8090
Fax: 215-925-0811

Resources for viewing hitched horsehair:

National Cowboy Hall of Fame
1700 Northeast 63rd Street
Oklahoma City, OK 73111
Tel: 405-478-2250

Pierre G. Bovis
The Az-Tex Cowboy Trading Company
P.O. Box 13345
Tucson, AZ 85732
Tel: 520-318-9512

Resource Books

Cowboy Culture – The Last Frontier of American Antiques by Michael Friedman
    P.O. Box 9, Rowayton, CT 06850

Cowboy Gear by David R. Stoecklein
    Stoecklein Publishing, P.O. Box 856, Ketchum, ID 83340 1-800-727-5191

Old Cowboy Saddles and Spurs by Dan and Sebie Hutchins

Tools of the Cowboy Trade: Today's Crafters of Saddles, Bits, Spurs & Trappings
    by Casey Beard, photographed by Dale DeGabriele. Available from Gibbs Smith, Publisher, P.O. Box 667, Layton, UT 84041, or call 1-800-748-5439 to order.

Glossary

Actual hitched blank: What is really hitched, put in the press, and nothing has been cut off.

Add: Lay a pull under the string with one end up. This pull will be ready to hitch in the next row. Leave 2 inches of pull down next to dowel to prevent hair from unraveling.

Apex: The outermost point of the diamond. When hitching a 6 row diamond, it is Row 7.

Back: The back of a hitched item. No pattern is on the back. The start point is usually on the back.

Background: The pulls which surround the pattern colors, usually all black or all white.

Billets: Leather ends.

Blank: The hitched part of an item.

Building a diamond: Hitching the whole diamond pattern from start to finish.

Bundle: Horsehair sold by the pound or partial pounds and tied together with string. Cleaned, sorted, and cut to length.

Button: Another term for the traditional knot covering joints.

Center: In reference to a belt. The very center of a belt pattern should be in the middle of a person's back.

Center hole: The ideal hole where the belt buckle should hook into. Belt sizes are measured from the foldover to the center hole. The center hole is in the tongue end of the billet.

Closed hitch: A knot. One of the 2 knots used in hitching.

Cover strip: Thin piece of leather covering joint where hitched blank and leather ends are sewn together.

Cross hitch: Pulls are crossed over each other. Take second pull and hitch it first. Then hitch the first pull over top of the second pull. This crosses the pulls, and creates a *barbershop pole* effect. Usually used on a border. If this is an open hitch row, open hitch the pulls; if it is a closed hitch row, close hitch the pulls.

Drop: The pull is put under the string and lays along the dowel. It is not hitched.

Face pulls: The front of the belt, hatband, etc., where the pattern is.

Finished hitched blank: Hitched horsehair that is sewn to leather ends.

Foldover: The leather billet end where the belt buckle is attached. The leather is folded over so the buckle can be attached. Belt sizes are measured from the foldover to the center hole.

Going into a diamond: Increasing the diamond pattern from the tip, or the start, to the apex of the diamond.

Going out of a diamond: Decreasing the diamond pattern from the apex to the end, or bottom, of the diamond.

Hitched blank: The hitched part of an item.

Hitching: A series of horsehair pulls knotted over string.

Hitching tension: The tightness of the hitched rows. Usually 8 ½ to 10 ½ rows per inch of hitching.

Horsehair knot: See knot.

In the round pattern: A pattern which goes all the way around the hitched item.

Knot: Also called horsehair knot or button. Covers areas where items are sewn or glued. A traditional technique using a needle and either horsehair pulls or thread.

Open hitch: A knot. One of the 2 knots used in hitching.

Pattern: The decorative colors in the hitched item.

Press: noun: Two pieces of steel, with nuts and bolts. Used to flatten the hitched tube. Verb: Putting the hitched tube in the press, as in *press the belt*.

Pull: Individual hairs twisted together in a strand. Usually 10 hairs per strand of black or gray colors; and 11 hairs per strand of white color.

Reading graph paper: Looking at the pattern on graph paper, and knowing when to drop, add, stand, open hitch, or close hitch. It is literally *reading* from left to right, top to bottom, and knowing what to do with each colored line and background pull on the paper.

Snug up: Pulling tightly on each individual pull before hitching it. This lays the pulls flatter in the previous row.

Stand: Nothing is done with the pull in that row. It sticks up in the air, and is always dropped in the next row.

Start point: The first pull on the string. It is the starting counting point of each row. This pull marks where the open or close hitches start in each row. Usually on the backside of the hitched object. It is identified in some way; either a different color, or piece of tape or double knot on the end.

Tongue end: Part of leather billet with 5 holes punched for belt buckle to hook into.

Tube: The round shape the hitching is in after coming off the dowel and before being pressed.

Index

6 row diamond, 7, 27, 41, 71, 73

A
Add, 21-23, 40, 72
Apex, 29, 78

B
Background, 75, 79-80
Beeswax, 87, 93
Belts, 51, 109
Bracelets, 49, 169
Buckles, 52, 55
Bundles, 9-10
Buying tips, 119

C
Cane, 5, 102, 169
Chicago screws, 89, 114
Close hitch, 13, 17, 23, 70, 73
Colors, 12, 21, 23, 38, 99, 121
Cowboys, 5, 117
Cross hitch, 7, 39

D
Diamond, 27, 82
Dowel, 13-14, 16, 20, 40, 47, 49, 107
Drop, 24-25, 40, 73
Dye, 35, 106

E
Earrings, 49
Eyes, 95
Face pulls, 74, 121
Foldover, 89, 114

G
Graph paper, 69, 121, 169

H
Hatbands, 48, 56, 63
Headstalls, 48, 102, 111, 169
History, 117
Hitched blanks, 53, 61-62, 87, 97

Hitching, 13, 17
Horsehair, 5, 9

I
In the round, 169
Inlays, 49, 107
Inspiration, 101

J
Joint, 88-89

K
Keepers, 55-56, 90
Key fobs, 7, 13, 59, 93
Knots, 93, 111

L
Leather, 51, 59, 83, 112

M
Magnetic board, 69, 78
Moors, 5, 117

O
Open hitch, 13, 17, 22, 27, 70, 73

P
Patterns, 70, 80, 100, 121
Peroxide, 35
Pictorials, 6, 180
Press, 7, 61, 103, 108
Prison, 5, 117, 179
Pulls, 5, 9-11, 13, 15, 24, 47, 78, 97

R
Reins, 48, 111
Restoration, 120
Rope, 48, 111, 169

S
Sizing, 51
Slider knots, 98
Spiral, 13, 19, 78
Stand, 25-26, 72

Start point, 15, 108
Sterling silver, 106, 180
String, 13-14
Suppliers, 181

T

Tails, 64-66

Tassels, 67, 114-115
Tube, 7, 104

W

Water, 32, 104, 108, 115

Notes

Notes

Order Form

Additional copies of *Hitched Horsehair: The Complete Guide for Self-Learning* may be obtained from River Publishing, P.O. Box 1123, Kettle Falls, WA 99141 U.S.A. Tel: (509) 738-6944.

Please send $25.95, plus shipping, by check or money order. Credit cards are not accepted. U.S. dollars please.

Inquire for wholesale prices.

Washington State residents add 7.5% sales tax.

Shipping:
- Within the U.S. - $4.00
- Canada - $5.00
- Mexico - $6.00
- Western Hemisphere - $8.00
- Europe - $11.00
- Asia & Africa - $13.00
- Pacific Rim -- $14.00

Name: _____

Address: _____

City: _____ State: _____ Zip code: _____

Telephone: _____